Storybook Toys

sew 16 projects from once upon a time

jill hamor

dolls,
puppets,
softies
& more

stashBOOKS®
an imprint of C&T Publishing

Text copyright © 2012 by Jill Hamor

Photography and Artwork copyright © 2012 by C&T Publishing, Inc.

Publisher: Amy Marson

Creative Director: Gailen Runge

Art Director/Book Designer: Kristy Zacharias

Editor: Lynn Koolish

Technical Editors: Carolyn Aune and Mary E. Flynn

Production Coordinator: Jenny Davis

Production Editor: Alice Mace Nakanishi

Illustrator: Zinnia Heinzmann

Photography by Christina Carty-Francis and Diane Pedersen of
C&T Publishing, Inc., unless otherwise noted

Published by Stash Books, an imprint of C&T Publishing, Inc.,
P.O. Box 1456, Lafayette, CA 94549

Library of Congress Cataloging-in-Publication Data

Hamor, Jill, 1972-

Storybook toys : sew 16 projects from once upon a time - dolls, puppets,
softies & more / Jill Hamor.

pages cm

ISBN 978-1-60705-550-1 (soft cover)

1. Soft toy making--Patterns. I. Title.

TT174.3.H39 2012

745.592'4--dc23

2012015423

Printed in China

10 9 8 7 6 5 4 3 2 1

Dedication

To my mother and my aunt Judy
for inspiring me as a child, and
to my three daughters for continuing to inspire me as an adult.

Acknowledgments

This book would not have been possible without the love and support of my husband. Thank you, Tom.

Special thanks to Susanne Woods, for her encouragement, and all the wonderfully talented people at Stash Books who were integral to this process, including but not limited to Amy Marson, Lynn Koolish, Gailen Runge, Alice Mace Nakanishi, Jenny Davis, and Kristy Zacharias. Much praise also to Christina Carty-Francis and Diane Pedersen for the beautiful photographs, and Zinnia Heinzmann for her work on the illustrations.

I am especially grateful and indebted to Carolyn Aune, my technical editor. I could not have done this without you! Your feedback and assistance have been invaluable.

Last, but not least, thank you to my pattern testers and helpers: Beth Webber, Genia Orlova, Lori Hamor, Audrey Hemesath, Simi Denson, and Andrea Maayeh.

contents

Projects

preface

Ten years ago, I would never have imagined I would be writing a sewing book about dolls and toys. I was busy working at an office full time and had never used a sewing machine. After my oldest daughter's first birthday I took a break from my first career to begin my second, at home, raising my kids. During this time of bleary-eyed joy and sleepless nights I found myself, like many others in this position, yearning for a creative outlet.

When I took up being a stay-at-home mom I thought about drawing, a childhood passion, but then considered learning how to sew because it seemed like a more practical choice. I purchased an inexpensive sewing machine and started following various sewing blogs and message boards to learn about fabric, patterns, and sewing techniques, and gather inspiration from the many creative talents online.

Around the same time, my older sister made a doll for my daughter. I was especially touched, and naturally I thought back to our childhood and a topsy-turvy Goldilocks doll that our mother had made for us. I remember with vivid detail every feature of that doll, from Goldilocks' pale butter-yellow cotton yarn hair and ice-blue embroidered eyes to her floppy arms and neck. Mama Bear's red gingham dress and Papa's pale blue denim overalls are crisply etched in my mind. I can almost feel the bears' dark brown fur and can picture perfectly the exact shape and size of their features. I remember being in awe of that doll and thinking it was one of a kind because *my mom* had made it. I was equally impressed by my sister's handwork, but ultimately the love and time put into making the toy is the gift that truly resonates most with me.

It wasn't long before I made my first doll from a popular Waldorf pattern and began my own toymaking hobby. I made several more dolls and toys from my own and others' basic patterns before discovering vintage doll patterns from the 1940s. I loved the nostalgic look and feel of these dolls. After sewing some of the old (and sometimes finicky) patterns, I eventually decided to draft one of my own, incorporating various features that I preferred. This pattern was the first version of *Sadie, Mae, and Elsie* (pages 58–69).

Over the past few years, I have received countless requests for this pattern and general doll-making advice. While eager to share the pattern here, I'm equally excited to share fifteen additional projects that I feel complement the doll and provide a sweet, vintage-inspired collection of toys. May they lead to fond memories for the little ones in your life!

introduction

In this book you will find a collection of sixteen projects that are reminiscent of some of my favorite handmade, mid-century toys. All the projects were inspired by toys depicted in vintage greeting cards, children's picture books, photographs of old toys, or images of vintage toy patterns.

This book is organized into five sections:

- **Tools and Techniques** highlights general information and sewing basics.

- **Illustrated Hand-Stitch Glossary** provides a quick reference for the hand stitches used.

- **All About Faces and Hair** covers more in-depth techniques for faces and hair that can be applied à la carte to the later projects.

- **Dolls** contains eight doll projects, including dolls for all sewing levels.

- **Toys** includes eight nostalgic toys, including a pajama bag, a roly-poly duck, and a sweet cuddly bunny.

Although many of these toys take several hours of work, there is something for everyone. Projects such as *Cottontail, Spot,* and *Humpty* can be finished in an evening, while others—such as *Sadie, Mae, and Elsie;* the *Jack and Jill Marionettes;* and *Topsy-Turvy Goldilocks and the Three Bears*—will take a few days to complete. The end result, however, is worth the effort; you will have personally created an heirloom-quality toy to be passed down for generations to enjoy.

While detailed instructions are included for each project (for those who prefer to follow a pattern), I envision this book as a collection of ingredients to make and customize your own creations. There is a step-by-step section on customizing faces and hairstyles, and each project contains suggestions for alternative ways to construct each toy. These sections, called Variations, are just a sampling of the dolls and toys that are just waiting to be made. Use your imagination and, most of all, have fun!

how kids can help

As the mother of three young girls, I hear "Can I help?" quite often (while sewing—never when cleaning). Though sometimes it is cumbersome, I try my best to involve my girls in every toy-sewing project, even if their part is as simple as helping me stuff a doll or choosing what fabrics to use. Since the toys I make are mostly for my kids, it's especially helpful to have their input. Each project includes suggestions on involving children, so you can pass along your sewing skills to a new generation.

tools and techniques

This chapter highlights the tools and techniques suggested for completing the projects in this book. If you sew, you likely have almost all the tools and materials you need to start making a toy or two.

Tools

The following are some of the basic tools that you'll need to have on hand.

- Sewing machine—nothing fancy, just a basic sewing machine

- Scissors—craft scissors for paper, sharp scissors for fabric, and small scissors for detail work

- Tape measure

- Assorted pins and needles—for hand sewing and embroidery

- Iron

- Doll needles—extra-long needles, in sizes ranging from 3˝ to 7˝, for sewing through stuffed areas and accurately placing features

- Stuffing fork, knitting needle, wooden spoon, paintbrush (with bristles trimmed down to approximately ⅜˝), chopsticks, or other stuffing tool

- Water-soluble and air-erasable markers

- Thread—general-purpose sewing thread as well as upholstery thread for attaching limbs and hair, and stringing marionettes

- Seam ripper

Optional, but recommended:

- Freezer paper

- Hemostats—a surgical tool with alligator teeth and a locking handle, useful for stuffing hard-to-reach areas and turning doll parts right side out

- Lightbox

- Pinking shears—useful for finishing seam allowances

Selecting Materials

See Resources (page 160) for more information on materials.

Children's toys use such small amounts of fabric, felt, yarn, and floss that one need not look far or invest much to have the materials necessary to make toys. Because of their size, many of the dolls in this book can be made using less than half a yard of cotton fabric. It is likely that you have scraps of fabric and bits of yarn that are perfect for several projects in this book.

Even if you have no materials on hand, you can purchase all the supplies needed to make a special toy or two at little cost.

Fabric

There are many suitable woven cotton fabrics, including muslin, that can be used for doll bodies. Look for a fabric with a tight weave and a color that appeals to you. My preferred fabric is Kona Cotton by Robert Kaufman. The colors that I typically use for bodies are Sand, Tan, Wheat, and Earth. For some of the other toys, quality corduroy (Spot, page 116) or cotton velour or Minky (Cottontail, page 112) fabrics are recommended.

Most of the dolls' clothes and the other toys in this book are made with such small amounts of fabric that you are likely to find the perfect fabric in your scrap bin.

> **tip** I often discover bits of fabric for toy-making while sorting through my daughters' outgrown clothes. While many of these garments are quite worn, having been passed down through at least three kids, I still have a hard time parting with some for sentimental reasons. Yet even old clothes that are no longer wearable often have some fabric that is ideal for repurposing into doll clothing or a small toy. Use the money you have saved by repurposing to purchase sheets of wool felt, luxurious yarns, and wool stuffing.

Felt

A colorful stash of wool felt (even scraps!) is a wonderful resource to have on hand. Wool felt can be used for facial features, doll shoes, hair, clothes, and accessories. It is easy to sew on by hand or machine, does not fray, and is quite durable. It is well worth the investment to use a quality 100% wool or wool-blend felt rather than the acrylic felts available in most craft shops.

Yarn

I prefer the texture and volume that yarn provides as hair for a cloth doll. Moreover, I like the nostalgic feel. There are many types of yarn that can be used, and some work better than others. Yarn used on the dolls in this book is either 100% wool or a wool-mohair blend, unless otherwise noted. My favorite bulky-weight or worsted-weight yarn is Lamb's Pride yarn by Brown Sheep.

Stuffing

Several kinds of stuffing can be used for making toys. Considering the hours needed to complete some of these dolls, it is well worth it to use a high-quality stuffing. Nothing spoils a handmade doll or toy like an inadequate stuffing job or poorly chosen stuffing.

WOOL

Clean, carded wool is without a doubt my preferred fiber for stuffing. It is a natural fiber that packs beautifully and provides a warmth and weight to dolls and toys that is truly unmatchable. I suggest wool stuffing, at least for *Sadie, Mae, and Elsie;* the marionettes; Goldilocks; the Little Red Riding Hood puppets; and the cone puppet.

POLYESTER

Polyester stuffing is a synthetic fiber that is relatively inexpensive and readily available at most craft and fabric stores. In general I have found that the most common brands at craft stores are either a really soft, squishy fiber, or a coarser, rougher type. Squeeze the packages and you should be able to tell the difference. I *do not* recommend the soft, squishy fiber for any of the projects listed above, which require a fiber that can be packed into the contoured face. However, a soft stuffing would be suitable for *Little Cub* (page 44), *Mary Lou* (page 48), or even *Small Fry* (page 52), and perhaps a few other toys in this book such as *Cottontail* (page 112), *Spot* (page 116), or *Henry* (page 121).

COTTON, BAMBOO, AND OTHER STUFFING

Other materials can be used as stuffing, including cotton, hemp, and bamboo fibers, and even stuffing made from corn sugar. If you are new to toymaking, test out different types of stuffing to find the kind that you like working with and that best serves your needs.

Preparing Patterns

All the patterns included in this book are full size, include seam allowances, and can be traced directly from the patterns located at the back of the book and on the pattern pullouts. When using the patterns, do not cut them but instead make templates (below) and cut the templates. This will keep the original patterns intact so that they can be used over and over again. Transfer all pattern markings to the template, including facial features, darts, arrows, cutting directions, and any other information noted on the pattern sheet.

Freezer-Paper Templates

I highly recommend using freezer-paper templates. Freezer paper can be purchased in a large roll from the grocery store, or in sheets that can be loaded directly into your printer, making the task of tracing patterns so much easier—simply scan and print. Freezer paper is inexpensive and patterns made from it can be used several times before you need to trace or print new ones.

Trace or copy the template pattern onto the paper (dull) side of the freezer paper.

Freezer-paper templates can then be ironed directly onto the right or wrong side of the fabric, eliminating the need for pins when cutting the patterns out of fabric.

Cutting

Place the cut-out freezer-paper template shiny side down on the fabric. Make sure to align the arrow on the pattern (if provided) with the grain of the fabric, which runs parallel to the selvage. Press with a hot iron (no steam) to adhere the template to the fabric. Pay close attention to the grain of the fabric—pattern pieces not cut appropriately may result in a distorted outcome.

If you are cutting on folded fabric or using a fabric without a right and wrong side, you can cut as you like; otherwise, make sure to reverse the pattern pieces so as to make a pair of arms, legs, ears, or pieces of clothing (sleeves, shorts, and so on). Pattern pieces that need to be cut in pairs are marked with a notation such as "Cut 1 and 1 reverse."

Transferring Pattern Marks

After the fabric patterns are cut, transfer pattern marks from the paper templates to the fabric pieces. Sometimes this can be done prior to peeling the freezer-paper pattern off the fabric. Other times, when the marks must be reversed, the freezer paper will need to be peeled off first and the fabric put on top of it. In either case, place the pattern, paper side down, on a lightbox or up against a window, with the fabric on top, so you can see through the fabric. Transfer all pattern markings to the fabric using an air-erasable or water-soluble marker. Refer to each project for specific instructions on transferring pattern marks.

Basic Sewing

With adequate time and a bit of patience, anyone with basic sewing skills should be able to tackle these projects. Below are some tips for sewing the toys in this book. Consult your favorite sewing book or look online for more detailed information about various sewing techniques.

- Use a shorter-than-normal stitch length (1.5mm) and high-quality thread when sewing doll bodies.

- Always choose the appropriate size needle (big enough so that you can thread it, strong enough to sew through the fabric, and small enough that it doesn't leave a big hole).

- Use a presser foot that allows you to easily see what you are sewing (such as an open foot).

- Sew seams twice for added durability, especially those places where seams will be stressed when stuffing, such as around a doll's neck and face.

- For sewing more complicated pieces, such as small fingers, follow a hand-drawn stitch line rather than use the edge of the fabric as a guideline. I find doing this helpful, especially if I'm trying to sew two identical seams with curves, such as the front seams of a doll's face.

- Sew darts with right sides together, starting from the widest part of the dart and finishing at the point. Backstitch to secure the stitching.

- Use pinking shears to trim and finish seam allowances to prevent unraveling of the raw edge of the fabric. Depending on the size of the toy, sometimes using pinking shears avoids the need to clip curves altogether.

- Make sure to clip and notch curves! This is especially important with stuffed toys. Clipping into the seam allowances of outward curves permits the edges to spread when the item is turned right side out. Likewise, notching the seam allowances on inward curves allows the edges to draw in when the item is turned right side out.

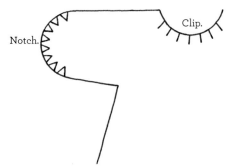

Clip or notch seams to avoid puckering.

Sewing with Knits

Some of the projects in this book call for knit fabric such as velour or sherpa. When sewing on knits, keep the following in mind:

- Use a long stitch length (2.5–3mm).

- Reduce the pressure on your sewing machine's presser foot, if necessary.

- Experiment with a walking foot (test ahead with scraps).

- Refer to your sewing machine's manual for added instruction and choose a needle suitable for sewing with knits (such as a ball point needle).

tip Using light- or medium-weight nonwoven fusible interfacing makes sewing with velour more manageable and helps prevent the edges from curling. Fuse the interfacing to the wrong side of the velour fabric prior to cutting pattern pieces. Always test first on scraps of fabric.

Stuffing and Finishing

Stuffing is a time-consuming process, but taking the time to stuff properly is well worth the effort. A poor job of stuffing can greatly affect a toy's finished appearance. For better stuffing results, follow these basic tips:

- Work with small pieces of stuffing to produce fewer lumps.

- Stuff fingers and extremities first. Use a pair of hemostats or a stuffing fork for hard-to-reach areas.

- Stuff and then stuff some more. Pack the stuffing tightly with a stuffing tool, such as the end of a wooden spoon, a wooden knitting needle, the end of a pencil or dowel, or even a paintbrush with the brush clipped down.

- When you are finished stuffing, close the openings with a ladder stitch (page 14).

tip An easy method to weight a doll or toy is to use sand. Most craft or hobby stores sell fine-particle sand that is inexpensive and works quite well for this purpose. Sew a small cloth pouch on three sides (double-sew the seams to be safe) and fill with sand. Make sure to securely sew the pouch opening closed. Nestle the bag in wool stuffing and place inside the doll or toy. Secure the sand pouch with more stuffing, as needed.

SAFETY *It is important to ensure that toys are safe in the hands of a young child. In particular watch out for buttons or other small objects that small children can pull off and swallow.*

making bias tape

For ¼˝-wide finished bias tape, cut the bias strips 1˝ wide. Fold and press the edges of the bias tape to the center. Then fold and press the tape in half.

illustrated hand-stitch glossary

Hand-Sewing Stitches

Basting Stitch

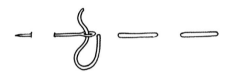

Ladder Stitch

Running Stitch

Whipstitch

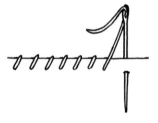

Backstitch

Blind Stitch

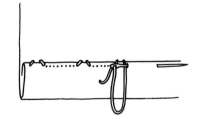

Embroidery Stitches

Blanket Stitch

Chain Stitch

Cross-Stitch

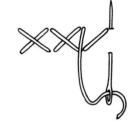

Stem Stitch

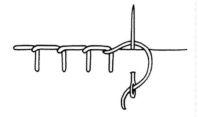

Outline Stitch

Satin Stitch

French Knot

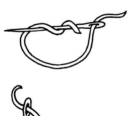

Long-and-Short Stitch

Lazy Daisy Stitch

all about faces and hair

My favorite part of making dolls is working on faces and hair. Although time-consuming, this process is always filled with a bit of excitement; it is during this step that the doll's personality really starts to take shape. Subtle changes inevitably take place with each tiny stitch and strand of yarn.

Eyes, Noses, Mouths, and Expressions

A doll's face, without a doubt, truly brings the doll to life. Even the smallest details greatly enhance character: The slightest arch of an eyebrow can suggest curiosity or surprise; a softly angled mouth may hint at a sly grin; an open mouth may convey a wide smile, laughter, or surprise.

 To more accurately place facial features or even decide on what those features will be, wait to work on a doll's face until after the head has been completely stuffed. The only projects for which I would recommend finishing faces before the pattern pieces are sewn together are *Little Girl Purse* (page 101) and *Kitten Pillows* (page 98).

Decide on an Expression

Every project in this book includes a template pattern for the doll's face where needed and the recommended materials and techniques.

If you are new to doll making, you may want to use the template pattern provided and follow each project's instructions. If you have some experience making toys or simply like doing things your way, experiment and create a one-of-a-kind toy.

If you have an expression in mind, test it out on your doll's face (see Testing Facial Expressions, page 19) and move on to Transferring the Expression (page 19). If you are not sure of a design, there are many places to look for inspiration. The children around you, picture books, greeting cards, old embroidery patterns depicting kids (many of these can be found online), or even online images of vintage cloth dolls can be invaluable and inexpensive sources of inspiration.

To test out different expressions, sketch a few blank doll heads on paper (or trace the head shape on the next page) to experiment with eye, nose, and mouth styles as well as size and placement on the doll's face. The following illustrations depict four different expressions—just a sample of the endless combinations of features a doll can have.

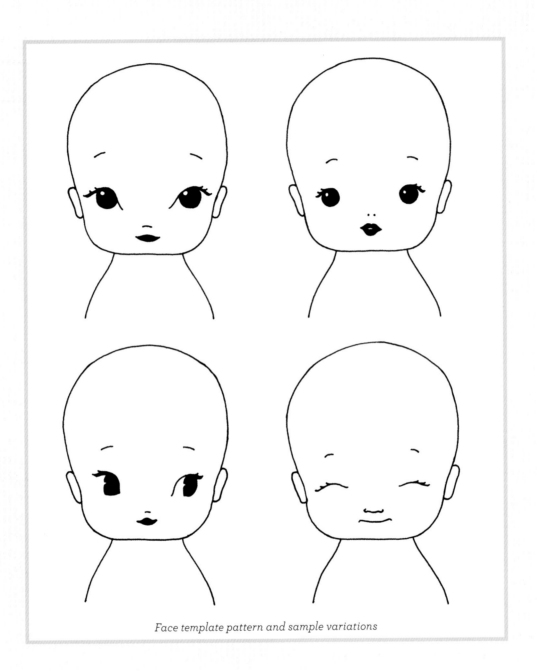

Face template pattern and sample variations

Testing Facial Expressions

Test facial expressions on a small piece of a plastic, such as a sandwich bag or scrap of plastic sheeting. Use a permanent marker and first check to make sure the marker dries and does not smudge. Place the plastic scrap on your facial expression sketch, trace it with the marker, and then place the plastic on the doll's face (with the drawn-on side *facing you*, just to be safe). Move the plastic around to find the proper style, size, and placement of the facial features. Use a series of plastic scraps to move different eyes, noses, and mouths around until the facial expression is to your liking. A scrap of the doll fabric can also be used, using an air-erasable or water-soluble marker to trace the facial expression.

When you have the features you want, retrace the expression onto paper and use this as your own custom face template.

Transfer the Expression from Paper to Fabric

Place a small piece of lightweight, nonfusible interfacing on top of the provided face template or a template that you have created, and trace the face onto the interfacing using an air-erasable or water-soluble marker. A lightbox or window makes this step easier. Cut around the facial expression, leaving approximately ¼˝ around the features (the eyes, nose, and mouth should all be on one piece together for proper spacing). The interfacing should be semitransparent and provide enough visibility to place and accurately center the expression on the doll's head.

Pin the outer edges of the marked interfacing to hold it in place (simply push the pins into the doll's head). Use an air-erasable or water-soluble marker to retrace the facial expression directly on top of the doll's face. Press firmly and retrace the lines as needed (lift edges to check). The ink should eventually seep through. Remove the interfacing and fill in any sparse lines directly on the doll's face. If the features are crooked or simply not satisfactory, mist with water, wait for marks to disappear and fabric to dry, and repeat as necessary.

tip Use a piece of waste thread and take a tiny stitch to mark the placement of the nose before sewing pieces together. After the doll is stuffed, remove the thread, but mark this spot with an air-erasable or water-soluble marker. When transferring the provided face template pattern, align the nose on the template with the nose mark on the doll's face.

tip It is *always best* to test markers beforehand on scraps of the fabric you are working with. If an air-erasable marker has not disappeared sufficiently, a few mists with water do the trick. Be sure to erase marks before applying any heat!

Embroider, Appliqué, or Sew On Features

All but one of the faces for dolls and toys in this book are achieved through the use of embroidery floss, felt, needles, and thread. While this section focuses solely on the techniques used in this book, there are many other popular methods for creating a doll's facial features, including paints, gel pens, pencils, beads, and plastic or glass eyes. Experiment and use whichever methods you are most comfortable with.

EMBROIDERED FEATURES

Embroidery is my preferred method for all doll faces. Embroidery floss is readily available, and inexpensive, and it comes in a vivid assortment of colors. Embroidered features hold up well over time, particularly in the hands of young children, and do not pose the choking hazards that buttons or plastic eyes might for babies and toddlers (if not secured properly). An embroidered face can also be easily taken out and resewn (unlike painting); this can be as simple reworking a single stitch to as complicated as redoing a whole eye.

tip Presoak your embroidery floss! Based upon my experiences, some darker "colorfast" embroidery floss do bleed (*especially* dark browns and reds). Presoaking is simple and saves hours of work.

To presoak: Place floss in lukewarm soapy water. Swirl and let sit overnight. Rinse thoroughly with cold water. Place on paper towels and press out excess water. If there are signs of bleeding, soak again. Otherwise, let air dry, wind on a bobbin, and store.

Embroidered Facial Expression

The following are step-by-step instructions for embroidering the face template pattern provided for *Sadie, Mae, and Elsie* (pullout page P2). The techniques, however, can be applied to other dolls in the book.

I use six-strand embroidery floss for all doll faces; however, I generally stitch using a single strand of floss at a time. Although time-consuming, this method allows for more precision and detail. Experiment and discover what best suits your needs.

Nose

1. Choose an embroidery floss shade just slightly darker than the color of the doll, and separate a strand from an 18˝-long piece of 6-string floss.

2. Use a long doll needle and enter at the back of the doll's head. Exit where the ear will eventually be attached, leaving a 4˝ tail at the back of the head.

3. Take a small tack stitch at the ear, reenter near this stitch, and bring the needle out at an edge of the nose. Figure A.

4. Change over to an embroidery needle and take a series of small stem or outline stitches (page 15) to embroider the nose. Figure B.

5. Rethread the doll needle and take the floss from the edge of the nose to the other side of the head, where the opposite ear will be sewn.

6. Take a small tack stitch, reenter the head at the ear, and exit at the back of the head.

7. Trim the 2 excess threads at the back of the head.

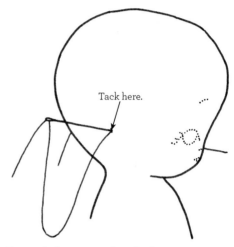

Tack here.

Figure A. Setup to embroider features

Figure B. Outline or stem stitch nose.

tip Hide knots by taking a tack stitch at the ear and exit at the back of the head. Tug slightly and cut the floss. As you gently pull up on the fabric, the floss tail should pull to the inside of the doll. All the tack stitches are located where the ears will later be sewn on, and the floss ends are inside the head.

Mouth

1. Thread a doll needle with a strand of red embroidery floss (separated from a generous arm's-length piece of 6-string floss). Follow Steps 2 and 3 (page 21), as detailed for the nose, and bring the needle out at a side of the mouth.

2. Change to a regular needle, and use a satin stitch (page 15) to embroider the mouth. When complete, rethread the doll needle and take the thread back through the head to the opposite side of the head, as you did for the nose.

Satin stitch mouth.

3. Follow Steps 6 and 7 of the instructions for the nose (page 21) to complete the mouth.

Eyes

1. Use a strand of brown, dark brown, or black floss (or other color of your choosing) to embroider the eyelash lines. Follow the steps as you did for the nose (page 21) and bring the floss out at the inner corner of the left eye (facing you).

2. Use an outline or stem stitch (page 15) to embroider the eyelash line. I often use a combination of both stitches, reversing the direction of the stitches at the top of the eyelash line. For example, for the left eye, I use an outline stitch from the inner eye corner to the top and then a stem stitch from the outer corner to the top. Experiment with stitches and find a technique that best suits you.

3. Fill in the outer part of the eyelash lines with additional stitches, if desired, to thicken the lash line. I generally fill in the outer part of the eyelash line a second time. This effect could also be achieved by initially using 2 strands of floss rather than a single strand (just for the outer part), but I have found that I can be much more precise using a strand at a time.

4. Take a few stitches for the 3 eyelashes on each side.

> **tip** When using a continuous piece of floss, redirect all embroidery floss between features by using the space where the ears will be sewn. I learned this the hard way: After simply moving the needle and thread from one eye to the other, I found that the embroidery floss was actually quite visible beneath the surface of the fabric!

5. Follow the steps as detailed for the nose to embroider the eyebrows, which are made from a series of small outline or stem stitches (reverse each side), much like the nose.

Eyelash line, eyebrow, and start of iris

tip When using darker fabrics for the doll's skin, the outer, white part of the eye can be either embroidered in white (using a satin stitch, page 15) or colored in using a white water-soluble pencil or paint. For the darker-skin-toned doll in *Sadie, Mae, and Elsie,* I used a white water-soluble pencil after embroidering the eyes.

6. For the iris, bring a strand of floss in the main eye color out near the center of the eye. Embroider around the iris by taking straight stitches from near the center of the iris to the outer edge of the iris and back to near the center. Leave a small area of fabric uncovered in the middle of the iris, generally about ⅛″. This area will provide an indentation to better sink the French knot pupil, rather than have the pupil sit atop a small mound of stitches. As the iris is filled in, this small patch of fabric will naturally get a bit smaller.

Fill in iris with different colors.

tip I generally use at least three shades of floss for the iris. Look closely at eyes, particularly if you are trying to replicate those of a child. Some eyes are much darker around the edges and lighter toward the middle or vice versa. Use stitches of varying lengths to replicate this look.

7. Sew the pupil using 4–6 strands of black embroidery floss or #5 perle cotton (2–3 strands or #8 perle cotton for the smaller dolls, such as the marionettes).

Using a long doll needle, follow Steps 1–3 for stitching the nose (page 21) and bring the floss out at the center of the iris. Make a French knot (page 15) and bring the needle back to where the opposite ear will be attached. Hold the knot in place until the floss has been pulled lightly taut at the side of the doll's head and the French knot looks secure. You may choose to pull back on the floss, which creates a more visible indentation in the eye line. Take a small tack stitch, reenter the head with the doll needle, and exit at the center of the other iris. Repeat the steps to make the second pupil.

8. To make the highlight, use 2–3 strands of white embroidery floss (1–2 for the smaller dolls) or perle cotton. Follow the steps above for the pupil, placing the highlight somewhere on the iris of each eye.

tip The eye highlight can be placed any-where on the iris. Moving it around changes the illusionary perspective of where light is reflecting off the eye. Use small white-headed pins to experiment with different perspectives.

To save time, or simply to achieve a different look, follow the steps above using only black embroidery floss for the eyes and eyebrows. See *Bedtime Storytelling Cone Puppet* (page 92) for an example.

> **tip** **A "Knotless" Start**
>
> If there is nowhere to hide embroidery knots, you can take a piece of thread and bend it in half. Thread the two ends into the needle. Take a tiny stitch where you will be embroidering, but don't pull the thread all the way through. Instead, bring the needle back through the thread loop that has not yet been pulled through the fabric, and pull. This will secure the thread. When you are finished embroidering, take a tiny tack stitch and bury the thread tails inside the doll.

APPLIQUÉD FEATURES

Eyes, noses, and mouths can be sewn on by hand or machine using wool felt or cotton material. Wool felt is my preference and is recommended for several projects in this book. Wool felt is easy to work with, does not fray, and offers the ability to easily test out facial expressions before sewing. In addition, with wool felt, unlike embroidery, what you see is what you get. Features can be sewn by hand before or after the toy is sewn together, or by machine before the toy is sewn together. See *Little Cub* (page 44), the wolf from *Little Red Riding Hood Puppet Set* (page 77), *Kitten Pillows* (page 98), *Cottontail* (page 112), *Spot* (page 116), or *Elephant Sewing Caddy* (page 125) for photographs of this technique.

SEWN-ON FEATURES

Buttons can be sewn on to create a doll's face. Most often, they are used for eyes. Buttons are simple to use and readily available, and they often provide a nostalgic charm all their own. That said, only *Henry* (page 121) calls for the optional use of buttons, though they (and likewise plastic or glass eyes) can be used for many other projects in this book. *Always be cautious of choking hazards,* however, when making a doll or stuffed toy for a child under the age of three (or for any child who may put things in his or her mouth) or make sure to use products that are labeled "child safe."

All About Hair

There are several techniques for making dolls' hair. Once you understand a few basic methods, however, it is easy to create custom hairstyles on your own with just a bit of patience, time, and imagination. The following is a guide to the techniques used for the projects in this book.

Method A: Pin, Wrap, and Secure Using Yarn

This is the primary technique I use for almost every doll. If sewn properly, the resulting hairstyles are secure and safe in the hands of young kids. Individually hand sewing each strand of yarn to the head admittedly takes time, but it ensures a durable hairstyle that can be built as you go.

tip **Yarn Hair Tips**

· Use upholstery or carpet thread that best matches the yarn hair color.

· Make sure to sew the yarn directly to the doll's head, not simply to the layer of yarn below it.

· For all hairstyles, keep in mind that the yarn will spring up a bit once sewn. Allow for extra length, as necessary.

· It is best to work on the hair after the facial expression is done but before the limbs have been sewn on. The ears should be sewn on already. The doll's head and torso should also be completely stuffed.

Method A involves the use of pins and a lot of hand sewing, but the end result is well worth the effort. Ponytails will be used to demonstrate the steps, which will be referred to in describing the other hairstyles to follow.

PONYTAILS AND BRAIDS

This method of making ponytails or braids is easiest using a bulky-weight yarn on a large doll head or worsted-weight yarn on a smaller-sized head. See *Sadie, Mae, and Elsie* (pages 58 and 64) for photos of these hairstyles. If the yarn you have chosen for a ponytail is thin, refer to the Method B section on Ponytails and Braids (page 37); Method A would be incredibly time-consuming for thin yarn.

Preparation

1. Move the yarn around the head and decide where to part the hair (side or center). For this example, the hair part will be on the side.

2. Place a pin where the top hair part meets the forehead hairline (white pin in the diagram) and place another pin at the back of this top hair part (yellow pin).

3. Place 3 more pins (green, blue, and purple) about ¼″–⅜″ apart between the yellow and white pins. The placement of these pins depends on the size of the doll's head and the weight of the yarn (the thicker the yarn, the farther apart you can space these pins). You will likely go back over with more yarn, so there is no need to fret about complete yarn coverage at this point.

tip I work with four pins at a time because it makes things manageable for me. Plus, it's easy for me to keep track of how many rounds of four I used to cover one side of the head so that I can make sure to use the same number of rounds on the opposite side. I don't want one ponytail bulkier than the other.

4. For a side hair part, place a pin at the top center of the head (red pin) as well.

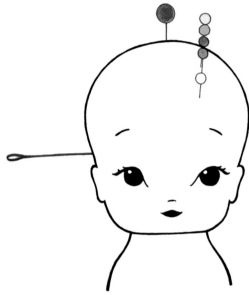

Pin setup for ponytails

5. Horizontally insert a long, thin doll needle behind the doll's ears approximately where the ponytails will later be fastened and secured.

6. Secure a dowel (or knitting needle or pencil) behind the doll's back with a piece of waste yarn or with 2 or 3 elastic hair bands knotted together. The placement of the dowel marks the length of the ponytails. Keep in mind that the yarn will spring up a bit when the hairstyle is complete.

tip A saddle-style doll stand is useful when working on doll hair. It is easiest to use this type of stand before the doll's arms and legs have been sewn on. See Resources (page 160) for more information. If not using a doll stand, place the doll torso in a clean coffee mug or other container to hold it upright and steady.

Wrapping

1. Working with a skein of yarn, leave a tail of yarn and wrap it once around the dowel. Bring the yarn over the doll needle, in front of the red pin, clockwise around the yellow pin, back behind and over the doll needle, down around the dowel, back behind and over the doll needle, up around the green pin, and so on until all 4 pins (yellow, green, blue, and purple) are wrapped with yarn.

2. Once the pins on top of the head and the dowel are wrapped with the yarn loops, wrap the yarn around the dowel a second time to temporarily hold it in place, and start to work on hand sewing the loops at the top of the head.

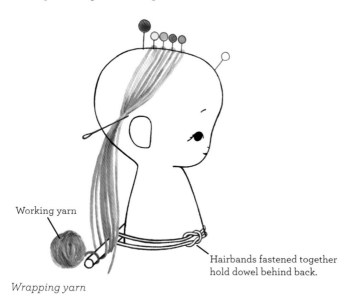

Working yarn

Hairbands fastened together hold dowel behind back.

Wrapping yarn

Securing

1. Thread a needle with upholstery thread and insert it near the back of the top hair part. Take a tack stitch and secure the thread in place near the yellow pin.

2. Remove the yellow pin, and take the needle and thread up through the loop of yarn. Take a small stitch through the doll's head, and then bring the needle and thread back through the loop of thread and pull tight to secure the loop and sew to the doll's head.

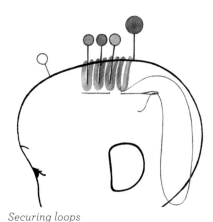

Securing loops

3. With the needle, reenter the doll's head at or next to the first secured yarn loop and exit at the second yarn loop (green pin).

4. Repeat Steps 2 and 3 until the first 4 loops are secured at the top of the head.

5. Position the 4 pins in place again further up the part, spaced the same distance as before. Slide the bottom part of the first 4 yarn loops off the dowel. Wrap the next 4 loops of yarn around the pins, doll needle, and dowel. Secure these loops as you did in Steps 2 and 3 above. Continue adding loops until the front of the hair part is reached (white pin). Do not cut the yarn.

6. Switch yarn to the other side of the head by running it across the head a few loops back from the front. Place the pins on the opposite side, beginning at the forehead, between the loops on the first side, not only for ease

in sewing but also for coverage. Reposition the doll needle behind the ear, and wrap and secure the loops in the same manner as before. As you work to the back of the top part, make sure to secure the piece of yarn brought over from the first side while simultaneously securing a loop on the second side.

Top part in hair

7. At the back of the top part, create a center back part by aligning the pins with the red pin. Start down the back of the head in the same manner. Wrap 4 pins, wrap around the doll needle (up and over on the back part, as shown in Step 2 on page 27), wrap around the dowel, and then sew and secure.

Ponytails, back hair part

Back part in hair

Filling In

Repeat at the very least on top of the head to fill in any sparse areas and to give more bulk so the hair can be styled. Keep in mind that the thicker the yarn, the bigger the ponytails and the bulkier the braids.

Making Ponytails or Braids

1. Once the head is sufficiently covered, cut the yarn on the opposite side from the starting tail. The starting tail should be on the first side, the end tail on the other. Trim both tails slightly shorter than the loops of yarn. When the hair is styled, these tails will not be visible because they are worked into the braid or ponytail.

2. For ponytails, comb through the loops on the first side of the head with your fingers, gather in an elastic hair band or braid, and then fasten. Repeat on the opposite side of the head.

Use a long doll needle and carpet thread to sew the ponytails securely to the side of the head, going through the hair bands and back through the doll head to the other side. Repeat this step until the ponytails are secure.

3. For braids, cut the loops and then braid the strands, fastening the ends of the braids with a small elastic hair band. Trim the excess yarn evenly. Anchor a few of the strands on the underside of the braid, just behind the ear, with a few stitches.

Waste string

BUNS AND BRAIDED LOOPS

Buns placed either high or low on the head can be made using Method A.

1. For lower placement behind the ear, arrange the pins at the top of the head as described for ponytails (Preparation, Steps 1–4, page 26). Thread 2 needles (a regular needle and a doll needle) with upholstery thread. Secure the threaded regular needle with a few tack stitches at the top hair part. Secure the threaded doll needle where the buns will be located and place the needle as shown. Figure A.

2. Rather than wrapping the yarn around a dowel (as for ponytails), wrap from the pins at the top of the head down around the *threaded doll needle* that is placed near the eventual location of the buns.

3. Working with 4 loops at a time and the threaded regular needle, sew down individual loops at the top of the head following Securing, Steps 2–4, of Ponytails and Braids (pages 27 and 28).

4. Bring the threaded doll needle up through the *bottom end* of all 4 loops and secure the loops together at the side of the head. Since the yarn loops are wrapped around this doll needle, you should be able to remove the needle from the head and the thread will already be holding all the loops. Simply secure in place with a tack stitch. Figure B.

5. Once the small bundle of loops has been securely sewn at the side of the head, adjust the doll needle, rotating it slightly around a quarter-sized section. The quarter-sized section at the side of the head will gradually fill in with hair, but there should still remain a slight indentation where the buns can later be anchored.

Continue adding loops in groups of 4 until the entire top part is covered.

For higher placement on the head (see darker-skinned *Sadie, Mae, and Elsie* doll, page 61), place pins and sew down loops from the center part, and then continue along the hairline, across the forehead and down the front of the face, up over the ears, and then down the back of the head. Figure C.

When you are finished, but before the buns are sewn on, the doll's head should look as shown. Figures D and E.

6. Add buns, braided buns, a braided loop or several loops, a short or long bundle of yarn to become a ponytail, or curls.

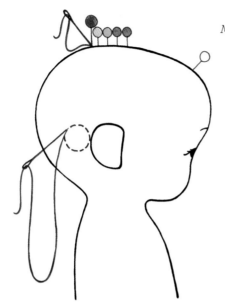

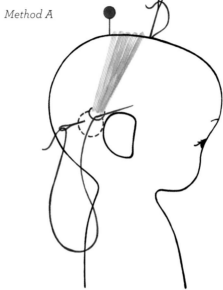

Method A

Figure A. Low bun pin placement

Figure B. Securing lower loops of low buns

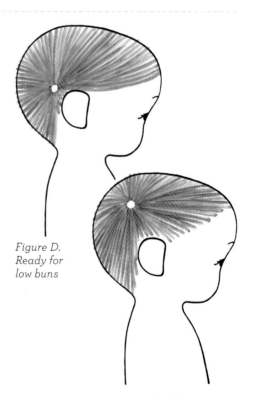

Figure C. High bun pin placement

Figure D. Ready for low buns

Figure E. Ready for high buns

How to Make Buns or Small Curls

1. To make buns, wrap yarn around a piece of cardboard. The number of wraps and the size of the cardboard depend on the weight of the yarn and the desired size of the buns. For example, I wrapped 10 loops around a 24˝ board for each of Mae's buns.

2. With carpet thread secured to the uncovered spot of fabric left for the buns, secure all the loops on an end of the bundle to the doll's head.

3. Use your finger to hold all the loops together on the other end (A) and twist until the bundle of loops starts to coil upon itself.

4. Wind it around itself, creating a twisted bun.

5. Keep your finger hooked inside the twisted bundle (A) and use your finger to guide the needle and thread through all the loop ends.

6. Sew the ends of the twisted loops tightly to the doll's head and then secure the bun in several places. Make sure the yarn is always secured to the doll's cloth head, not to the yarn beneath it, or the bun will likely come undone.

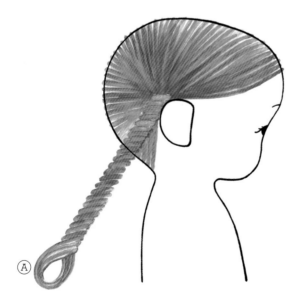

Twisting to make bun or small curls

Securing buns or small curls

GOLDILOCKS' HAIR

1. Follow the steps for ponytails for the top part of the doll's head (refer to Preparation, Wrapping, and Securing, pages 26–28). When you reach the back of the head, place pins perpendicular to the top part and work across the back of the head, wrapping and securing as for the top of the head. Figure A.

2. Once the head is sufficiently covered, finger comb through the loops and start to work with a bundle of approximately 4 loops at a time, depending on the weight of the yarn and your personal preference.

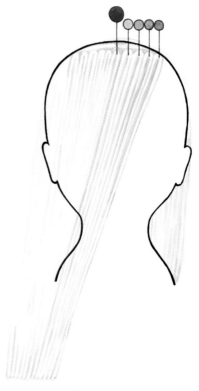

Figure A. Back of Goldilocks' head

3. Sew down the bundle at the ear line (A) with a small stitch or 2. Figure B.

4. Place a finger through the end of the 4-loop bundle (C) and twist.

5. Press down with your free hand at the center of the twisted bundle (bundle B) and bring C up to A, folding the bundle in half. As you are doing this, bundle B should start to twist itself. You can twist the bundle even more if desired (in the direction it naturally wants to go).

6. Bring the needle and thread through C and sew securely to the doll's head at A. Make sure the yarn is always secured to the doll's cloth head, not to the yarn beneath it, or the curls will likely come undone. Figure C.

7. Repeat until all the yarn is sewn into twisted bundles.

8. Secure the twisted bundles again on the underside of the curls, closer down toward the neckline, if desired.

A similar hairstyle could be achieved by making several individual small curls, from the ear line down toward the back of the neck, using Steps 4–6 of How to Make Buns or Small Curls (page 32).

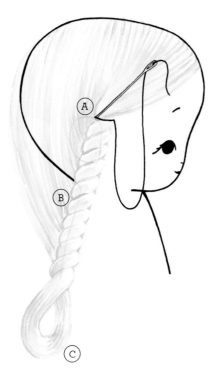

Figure B.

Figure C. One of Goldilocks' bundles is completed and a second is ready to be doubled and sewn into place.

LITTLE RED'S WRAPPED BRAIDS

1. Place pins similar to the placement described in Steps 1–5 for low-placed buns (page 30); however, leave an uncovered area across the top of the doll's head, where the braid will ultimately be placed. Secure the ends of all the front and back loops. Figure A.

2. After the yarn is sewn down, measure from the center base of the neck, up over the top of the head, and back to the base. Place a bundle of yarn slightly more than twice the measured length on a table. (How much yarn is in the bundle depends on the weight of the yarn. For Little Red, I used 15 strands of bulky-weight yarn.) Tie the bundle at the center using a piece of matching yarn. Knot and trim the tie.

3. Braid from the center of this yarn bundle to one end, and then from the center to the other end, creating a braid on each side of the center knot that is the length of the distance measured above. (To make the process easier, the bundle of yarn can be centered over a wall hook or similar feature, and then braided down on either side.) Secure the ends with small invisible elastic bands and trim the yarn ends evenly.

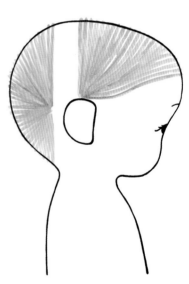

Figure A. Little Red's braids

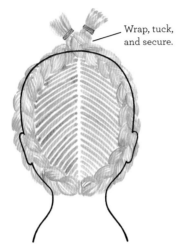

Wrap, tuck, and secure.

Figure B. Attaching Little Red's braids

4. Using upholstery or other strong, coordinating thread, center and securely sew the middle center knot of the braid to the base of the neck. Wrap the 2 braids up and over each other at the top of the head and secure the braid in various spots. Figure B.

A simpler technique to achieve this hairstyle is described under Method B (page 37). However, while undoubtedly more time-consuming, I prefer Method A for wrapped braids (actually, for almost every hairstyle!) because it provides more control over the ultimate look of the hairstyle. You build as you go. And if you are using a bulky yarn and do not want extra-bulky braids, simply attach a thinner braid.

BANGS

Use Method A to create bangs by placing pins straight across the hairline at the top of the forehead. Place a doll needle at the back center part. Wrap the yarn back and forth between the pins and the doll needle on top of the head. Secure loops across this line and add more loops right above it, if necessary. When finished, reposition and style the looped bangs along the front of the forehead. Cut the loops and trim the yarn.

Bangs can also be made by sewing a yarn wig (page 39).

Method B: Sew a Yarn Wig

The following is one of the more commonly used methods for rag-doll yarn hair. It involves winding yarn around a piece of stiff material (for example, cardboard or a hardback book cover) and then using a sewing machine to make a hair part that is then hand sewn to the doll's head. I'll go through the basic steps I use, but you will find that there are several variations of this technique. The steps below describe the process for ponytails or braids, though this method can be used for various hairstyles, described briefly in Sewn-Wig Variations (pages 38 and 39).

PONYTAILS AND BRAIDS

Take Measurements

1. Measure your doll's head from A to B— around the back of the head to the desired length of the ponytails.

2. Measure the length from C to D—the forehead hairline to the nape of the neck.

Ponytail measurement

Prepare the Wig

1. With a craft or utility knife, cut a piece of cardboard that is approximately twice the length of A to B and at least 2″ wider than the measurement from C to D.

2. Cut away a small strip of the board at least ⅝″ wide (wide enough for your sewing machine's presser foot) and at least the length of C to D. Either cut away this strip in the center of the piece of cardboard (for a center hair part) as shown below, or to the side for a side part. Leave the bottom 2″ of the cardboard intact to hold the board together.

3. Keeping the yarn strands snug against each other with just a slight bit of overlap (depending on the weight of the yarn), wrap the yarn around the board. The number of times you wrap the yarn around the board depends on the size of the doll's head and the weight of the yarn. Keep in mind that each time around the board is 2 pieces of yarn.

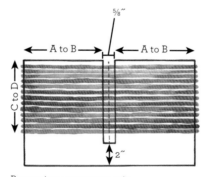

Preparing sewn-yarn wig

Sew a Part in the Hair

1. Place the yarn-wrapped cardboard under the sewing machine's presser foot and sew along the gap in the cardboard.

2. Slide the yarn off the cardboard and place the yarn wig on the doll's head.

3. Turn under the front and back edges of the wig just slightly, and securely hand sew it to the head along the machine-stitched part.

4. Cut the loops (*optional*) and style into ponytails or braids. Refer to Steps 2 and 3, Making Ponytails or Braids (page 29).

SEWN-WIG VARIATIONS

Wrapped Braids

Follow the instructions under Take Measurements (page 37); however, when determining the length of A to B, measure from the top of the head down, behind the base of the neck, then back up to the top of the head and over to the opposite ear (at least). This will ensure that you have enough yarn to braid and wrap. It is always safe to err on the side of having too much yarn (in length) because this can be easily fixed by trimming the braids to the desired length. Follow the instructions under Prepare the Wig (page 37) and Sew a Part in the Hair (at left). Once braids are complete, bring the braids around the base of the neck and then up on top of the head. Wrap around each other and secure.

Loose Hair

Follow the instructions under Take Measurements (page 37). The distance from A to B should be longer than the eventual length of the hair, which will be trimmed as a final step. Decide whether you want a center or side part. In either case you will make at least two different hair pieces. The length from C to D for this hairstyle will be the top center part. Another hair piece will be made to cover the back of the head. This is identified as E to F in Figures A and B.

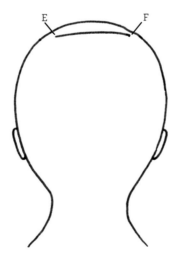

Figure A. Loose hair, back-of-head measurement

Figure B. Sewing down back hair piece, loose hair

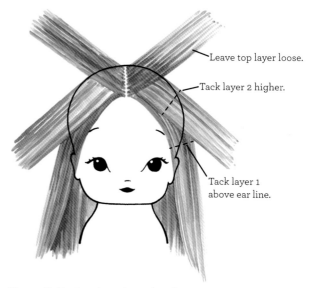

Leave top layer loose.

Tack layer 2 higher.

Tack layer 1 above ear line.

Figure C. Sewing down loose hair layers

Depending on the weight of the yarn, at least the first layer of yarn should be tacked down to the side of the head and another layer should be placed on top. Sew the additional layers of yarn, tacking where needed, to the side of the head. Make sure the yarn is sewn to the doll's cloth head and not simply to the yarn underneath. The top layer(s) of hair should not be secured anywhere except the hair part, giving the illusion of loose hair. Cut the loops and trim evenly. See Jill in *Jack and Jill Marionettes* (page 70) and *Bedtime Storytelling Cone Puppet* (page 92) for photos of this hairstyle. Figure C.

Bangs

Measure across the top of the forehead where the bangs will be sewn. Also measure the desired length of the bangs, and add at least an extra inch. Make a sewn-yarn wig for the bangs, using the steps outlined (page 37). Align the sewn part across the top of the forehead and secure the sewn-yarn bangs. Trim the bangs to the desired length.

Method C: Take the Yarn through the Head

This method works best with a flat or small doll head and a lightweight yarn. It involves sewing yarn directly through the head, often resulting in a very secure and neat finish. One drawback to this method, particularly if the yarn is too thick, is that it is hard to undo a hairstyle without some visible damage to the integrity of the doll's head. Speaking from experience, there will likely be several holes in the doll's cloth head covering (larger than those left by Methods A and B because the yarn is almost certainly thicker than carpet thread). And although these holes can usually be re-covered somewhat once a hairstyle is redone, it is only fair to mention this drawback.

To use this method, thread a doll needle with a very long arm's length of yarn and bring the needle and yarn directly through the head, back and forth, to achieve the desired hairstyle.

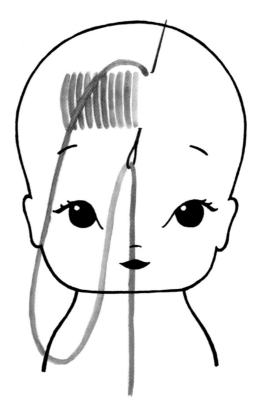

Sewn-on bangs

Method D: Embroider the Hair

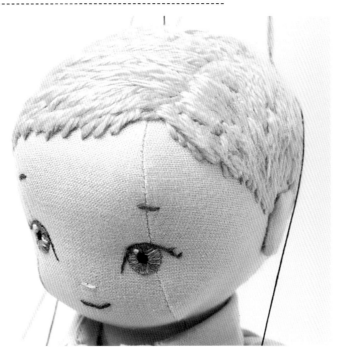

Hair can also be embroidered directly onto the head. It is easiest to use this method with thin yarn. Hair can be sewn onto the head using a series of small long-and-short stitches (page 15) to create a short hairstyle. Figure A.

Hair can also be embroidered using more elaborate embroidery stitches, including but not limited to outline stitch, stem stitch, or chain stitch (see Illustrated Hand-Stitch Glossary, pages 14 and 15). Combine stitches for a more customized look. Add small braids or ponytails once the head is sufficiently covered with embroidery stitches. See *Mary Lou* (page 48) for another example of this hairstyle technique.

Figure A. Embroidered hair

Alternative Methods

Besides using yarn, there are other materials and methods for adding hair (or the look of hair) to a doll. The following are a few of the more common methods used for the remaining dolls in this book.

PRE-ASSEMBLY SEWN-ON HAIRSTYLES

Felt, chenille, velour, or other assorted fabrics can be sewn directly onto the doll's head before sewing the head pieces together. Ponytails, braids, or buns can also be sewn from these materials and securely fastened when sewing the front and back of the head together, as in Little Girl Purse (page 101), which gives a more detailed description and a photograph of this process.

SEWN WIGS

This method involves actually sewing a wig out of felt, knit, or woven material that is then sewn onto the doll *after* the doll body has been sewn and stuffed. See Small Fry (page 52) for a more detailed description of this process.

Other Ways to Customize a Doll

There are countless additional ways to create a custom doll. Add freckles, birthmarks, or glasses for a more individual touch. Consider hairstyles made from ribbons, ruffles, or rickrack. Appliqué a heart with your name or initials and the date, or embroider a sweet signature somewhere on the doll's body. If you know how to crochet, there are several wonderful tutorials and techniques on the Internet for creating a crochet wig for a doll. The possibilities are endless!

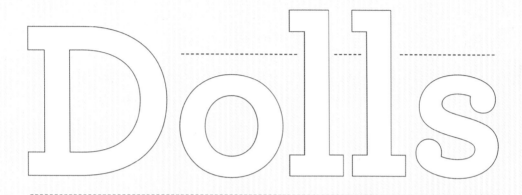

Dolls

The following eight projects represent a range of dolls reminiscent of hand-made cloth dolls from the 1940s and 50s. From rag dolls to a marionette puppet set, there are projects for all skill levels. You will find dolls here that will appeal to boys and girls and to adults who are young at heart.

Little Cub

Finished size: 14˝ tall

This awake-asleep baby is a sweet toy for any young child and an ideal project for any beginning toymaker. The cute bear hood provides coverage for the back side of the head so only one face is visible at once. With young children in mind, this project was designed to be machine washable and can be made using synthetic stuffing (no wool stuffing or wool yarn hair required!).

materials

½ yard furry fleece or cotton sherpa (fleecy cotton fabric) for sleeper and hood

⅜ yard or 2 pieces 8″ × 12″ cotton fabric for doll body

¼ yard or 8″ × 15″ piece cotton for hood lining

¼ yard or 8″ × 15″ piece lightweight fusible interfacing

½ yard tear-away stabilizer

Freezer paper

Embroidery floss for features

Wool felt scraps for eyes

Stuffing

Instructions

Make the Body

Both the front and back sides of Little Cub are identical, except for the facial features. Just change from asleep to awake by turning the hood around.

1. Cut out the body pieces and trace the stitching lines of the face and neck curves using a lightbox or window. (I find this helps to keep the sides symmetrical.) Mark the placement of the nose on both front and back pieces with a water-soluble marker or a piece of thread.

2. Pin the body pieces together and sew, using a ³/₁₆″ seam allowance. Leave an opening on the torso side, as indicated on the pattern piece.

notes:

- *Use the template patterns on pages 129, 130, and 133.*

- *Read all the project instructions before beginning the project.*

- *Refer to Tools and Techniques (pages 9–13) as needed.*

- *Trace all pattern pieces onto freezer paper (page 11).*

- *Pieces are sewn together with right sides facing, unless otherwise noted.*

- *Use a short stitch length for the body. Use a slightly longer stitch length for the sleeper.*

3. Trim the seam allowances and clip notches and curves, as necessary.

4. Turn the body right side out and stuff firmly. Refer to Stuffing and Finishing (page 13) for general tips about stuffing.

5. Close the opening using a ladder stitch (page 14).

Make the Sleeper

Note: In addition to lengthening the stitch, it is helpful to decrease the pressure on the presser foot when sewing on the thick fleece or sherpa. You might also find using a walking foot helpful.

1. Trace the sleeper on an 11″ × 12″ sheet of freezer paper. Do not cut the pattern out.

2. To prepare for sewing, cut and stack 2 pieces 11½″ × 12½″ sleeper fabric, right sides together. Press the shiny side of the freezer-paper sheet to the top layer of the fabric. You now have 2 layers of fabric with the freezer paper on top. Do not cut out the sleeper yet and do not remove the freezer paper.

3. Place this stack on top of a piece of tear-away stabilizer that is at least the size of the fabric. Pin all layers together securely.

4. Sew, following the pattern lines drawn on the freezer paper. Make sure to leave the straight top edge of the neck area open, as designated on the pattern.

5. Gently tear away the freezer paper and stabilizer and trim away the excess fabric, leaving ¼″–½″ seams. Clip the corners and notch the curves, if necessary.

6. Turn right side out and lightly stuff the feet and hands of the sleeper.

Make the Hood

1. Trace the ear pattern on a 4″ × 4″ piece of freezer paper. Follow Steps 2–5 for Make the Sleeper and sew 2 ears, leaving the straight bottom edge of each unsewn. Trim the seams and turn right side out.

2. Iron lightweight fusible interfacing to the fleece fabric prior to cutting out the hood pieces. Sew a dart in the back of the hood.

3. Position the ears on the back outer hood piece (see pattern for placement) and pin the front outer hood piece on top with right sides together (the ears are sandwiched between the layers).

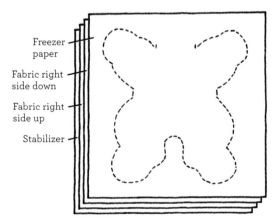

Freezer paper

Fabric right side down

Fabric right side up

Stabilizer

Sew sleeper.

4. Sew around the outer edge of the hood with a ¼″ seam allowance.

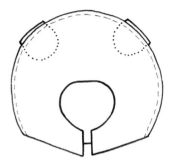

5. Sew the hood lining dart and sew the hood lining together around the outer curve only, with a ⅜″ seam allowance.

6. Pin the hood lining to the outer hood, right sides together, and sew all the way around with a ¼″ seam allowance, leaving a 2½″ opening at the center back edge of the hood for turning.

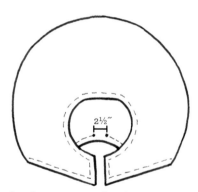

Sew lining to outer hood.

7. Trim the seams, clip the corners, and turn the hood right side out.

8. Add a child-safe closure to the hood bottom front edges. I used a no-sew snap fastener.

Finish the Doll

Place the Little Cub body inside the sleeper. The hands and feet should be only lightly stuffed and should move freely near the body.

Turn under the raw edges and hand sew the neck of the sleeper securely to the neck of the body using a ladder stitch (page 14). Embroider the facial features, referring to the provided template patterns as needed. If using wool felt for the awake side eyes, embroider the asleep side first and hide any knots where the felt circles will be sewn on the opposite side. Then cut 2 felt circles and whipstitch them in place. Add a French knot or 2 small parallel stitches as a highlight to each eye.

If you plan to embroider all the features (recommended if planning to machine wash), use a "knotless start" (Tip, page 24) and embroider the circles on the awake side with a satin stitch.

> ## how kids can help
>
> This is a project that can definitely use little hands to stuff, since it is hard to go wrong! Have your child help lightly stuff the hands and feet of the sleeper. An older child can help sew the furry neck to the doll body. The texture of the fleece is very forgiving and easily hides wayward small stitches.

Variations

As my youngest daughter suggested, the faces on these dolls can be more than just awake or asleep. What about happy or sad? Add a simple embroidered hairstyle (page 41) on both sides. Or alter the hood to make a wee piglet, monkey, bunny, or perhaps a little lamb.

Mary Lou

Finished size: 13˝ tall

Mary Lou is a basic rag doll that is entirely embroidered (including her undershorts!) except for her basic removable dress. Smaller and simpler than most other dolls in this book, Mary Lou is a perfect project for both beginners and those more experienced in toymaking: For beginners, its uncomplicated design makes it a perfect first project; and for the more experienced, it's a blank canvas for testing out some new embroidery techniques and experimenting with new fibers.

materials

⅓ yard or 2 pieces 10˝ × 10˝ cotton fabric for doll body, arms, and legs	Embroidery floss (array of colors for eyes, mouth, undershorts, and shoes)	Optional: Approximately 1 yard ¼˝-wide lace trim
⅓ yard or 1 piece 10˝ × 20˝ cotton fabric for doll dress	Alpaca or wool needlepoint yarn for doll hair	Small scraps of wool felt for flower
	Stuffing	Seed beads for shoes and decorative pin

Instructions

Make the Body

Even though Mary Lou has a slightly different body shape, follow Steps 2–5 in Make the Body of *Little Cub* (page 45) for instructions on sewing and stuffing the body. Refer to Stuffing and Finishing (page 13) for general tips about stuffing.

notes:

- *Use the template patterns on pages 131 and 132.*

- *Trace all pattern pieces onto freezer paper (page 11).*

- *Read all the project instructions before beginning the project.*

- *Refer to Tools and Techniques (pages 9–13) as needed.*

- *Press freezer-paper templates to the fabric and cut out the fabric pieces before removing the freezer-paper templates.*

- *Trace the face, hair, undershorts, and shoe templates onto the right side of the fabric pieces prior to sewing. Trace any stitching lines (to assist with sewing the head shape) on the wrong side of the fabric.*

- *Pieces are sewn together with right sides facing, unless otherwise noted.*

- *Use a short stitch length.*

- *The seam allowances are ³⁄₁₆˝, unless otherwise noted.*

Make the Arms

1. Pin 2 arm pieces together and sew, leaving the top of the arm open for turning.

2. Clip the curve around the hand, as necessary, and turn the arm right side out.

3. Stuff the arm, leaving the upper portion of the arm more lightly stuffed. Fold ½˝ of the top edge toward the inside and close the opening using a ladder stitch (page 14).

4. Sew the arm securely to the torso just under the neck curve. Be sure the thumbs face forward.

5. Repeat for the other arm.

Make the Legs

1. Pin 2 leg pieces together and sew, leaving the top of the leg open.

2. Clip the curve around the foot, as necessary, and turn the leg right side out.

3. Stuff the leg, leaving the upper portion of the leg more lightly stuffed. Fold ½˝ of the top edge toward the inside and close the opening using a ladder stitch.

4. Sew the leg securely to the base of the torso using a ladder stitch.

5. Repeat for the other leg.

Embroider Details

1. Refer to All About Faces and Hair (pages 17–42) for ideas on embroidering the face. A template pattern is provided, but this is a great project to test your skills. Hide all embroidery tack stitches at the eventual place-ment of the buns, and hide the tails of the floss inside the head.

2. Refer to the instructions for Method D: Embroider the Hair (page 41) and use a stem stitch (page 15) to embroider the hair, following the hairline marked on the template pattern, or use your own design. Refer to How to Make Buns or Small Curls (page 32) to create the buns shown on Mary Lou.

3. Use a satin stitch (page 15) to embroider Mary Lou's shoes. Using the lines on the leg pattern as your guide, sew vertical satin stitches from the top to the bottom seam of the foot. Do this on both the front and the back of the foot. Attach floss at a front side of the shoe, take it across to the other side, and attach it to create the strap. Sew 2 seed beads on each outer edge as the shoe's buttons (*optional*).

4. Create undershorts by outlining the shorts with a stem stitch and then adding lazy daisy (page 15) flowers or French knot (page 15) polka dots. Sew a bit of very narrow lace where the legs attach to the body to create the undershorts' leg lace (*optional*).

Sew the Doll Dress

1. Refer to the dress diagrams (page 65) if needed. Pin the front edge of the sleeve to the front of the dress and sew. Repeat for the other side.

2. Pin the back edge of the sleeve to the back of the dress and sew. Repeat for the other side.

3. Press ¼˝ under to form the hem on the sleeves and edgestitch, or apply bias tape.

4. Pin the front and the back of the dress together at the sides and sew the sleeve and side seams.

5. Fold the back raw edges ⅛˝ under, press, and then fold again ¼˝ and press.

6. Press a small center front pleat and tack to fit the dress snugly to the doll's neck.

7. Sew bias tape (page 13) around the neck edge or finish with a ⅛˝ hem or other decorative trim.

8. Unfold the bottom back edges. Press and sew a ¼˝ bottom hem.

9. Refold the back edges, and sew the back hems. Add 2 or 3 snaps or buttons and add trim to finish the bottom edge of the dress.

Finish the Doll

Add bows or other decorative accents to hair and clothes. I used two layers of felt cut into irregular circles with a few seed beads attached to make a little flower brooch for the dress.

how kids can help

Quick to sew, stuff, and assemble, Mary Lou dolls can be stitched up in batches and handed over to your little ones so you can see what they create! I have sewn a few of these dolls for my daughters and let them take over the rest of the doll's design. It is fun to watch what their imaginative minds dream up! This is also a wonderful opportunity to demonstrate a whole range of embroidery techniques and work hand in hand with your child to create a truly one-of-a-kind playmate.

Variations

Embroider socks or striped tights, or change up the shoe style. Experiment with facial expressions, or try out different decorative embroidery techniques or yarns to achieve a more elaborate hairstyle. The variations are limitless. This doll can be whatever you wish!

Small Fry

Finished size: 15˝ tall

With overalls that button, a shirt that snaps, and shoes that tie, this little lad is both fun and educational. The simple rag-doll construction can be easily adapted to make the perfect sidekick for boys or girls alike.

Instructions

Make the Body

Refer to Make the Body for *Little Cub* (page 45). Be sure to mark the nose placement for the face with an air-erasable or water-soluble marker (or a piece of waste string) on the right side of a pattern piece. Add a small bag of sand to weight the doll, if desired, prior to stuffing the torso (see Tip, page 13). Refer to Stuffing and Finishing (page 13) for general tips about stuffing.

notes:

- Use the template patterns on pages 133–137.

- Read all the project instructions before beginning the project.

- Refer to Tools and Techniques (pages 9–13) as needed.

- Refer to Sewing with Knits (page 13).

- Trace all pattern pieces onto freezer paper (page 11).

- Press pattern pieces onto the fabric and cut out the fabric pieces before removing the freezer-paper templates.

- If using velour, iron lightweight interfacing to the wrong side prior to cutting the hair pieces, if needed.

- Pieces are sewn together with right sides facing, unless otherwise noted.

- Use a short stitch length.

- The seam allowances are $^3/_{16}$˝, unless otherwise noted.

Make the Arms

1. Pin 2 arm pieces together and sew, leaving the top of the arm open.

2. Notch the curve around the hand, as necessary, and turn the arm right side out.

3. Stuff the arm, leaving the upper portion of the arm more lightly stuffed. Fold ½˝ of the top edge toward the inside and close the opening using a ladder stitch (page 14).

4. Sew the arm securely to Small Fry's torso just under the neck curve.

5. Repeat for the other arm.

Make the Legs

1. Pin 2 leg pieces together and sew, leaving the top of the leg open.

2. Notch the curve around the foot, as necessary, and turn the leg right side out.

3. Stuff the leg, leaving the upper portion of the leg more lightly stuffed. Fold ½˝ of the top edge toward the inside and close the opening using a ladder stitch.

4. Sew the leg securely to the base of Small Fry's torso using a ladder stitch.

5. Repeat for the other leg.

Embroider the Face

Refer to All About Faces and Hair (pages 17–24), and embroider the facial features using the provided face template pattern or a design of your own. The fabric wig will sufficiently cover any embroidery knots on the back of the head.

Sew a Fabric Wig

Note: Refer to Sewing with Knits (page 13).

1. Pin a wig front to a wig back and sew. This is the outer part of the sewn wig.

2. Pin the remaining wig front to the remaining wig back and sew, this time leaving an opening at the top as designated on the pattern. This is the inner part of the sewn wig.

Sew inner wig.

3. Turn the inner wig right side out and place inside of the outer wig, so that the right sides are facing.

4. Align the inner and outer wigs' side seams and the curves and corners of the wigs, and pin in place.

5. Starting at the back bottom center, sew completely around the front and back of the wig.

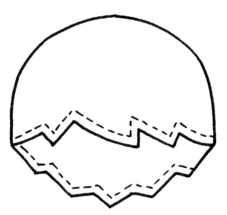

Sew inner and outer wigs together.

6. Clip the seam allowances and turn the wig right side out through the inner wig opening. Sew the opening closed using a ladder stitch.

7. Fit and adjust the wig onto the doll's head, and hand sew the wig in place. Take stitches approximately ¼˝ in from the edges on the *underside* layer of the wig so that the hair edges can lift from the head.

Make the Clothes

OVERALLS

1. Pin the overalls front and back together, and sew along the side seams. Repeat for the facing.

2. Pin the inner edges of the legs and sew. Clip the seam allowance around the curve.

3. Align and pin the overalls and the facing, and sew ⅛˝ all the way around the front top and the armholes. Leave the back top edge open. Clip the seam allowances and turn the overalls right side out.

4. Pin 2 overall strap pieces together and sew, leaving an end open. Clip the corners and turn the strap right side out. Repeat for the other strap. If you are using buttons as overall fasteners, make a buttonhole of the appropriate size at the finished end of each strap. If you are using snaps, place the bottom half of a snap on the finished end of each strap.

5. Fold inward the raw edges of the straight edge of the overall back, and press. Insert the unfinished edges of the overall straps on either side of the back opening. Pin and topstitch across the entire top edge, securing the straps in place.

6. Add buttons or the other half of the snap to the front of the overalls.

7. Press under approximately ½˝ (or make a smaller double-folded hem), pin, and topstitch down to create the hem at the bottom of each overall leg.

8. Add a pocket (*optional*). Cut a small rectangle of fabric (I cut mine 2˝ × 2½˝). Press a ³/₁₆˝ hem on all sides. Topstitch down the top edge of the pocket piece. Center the pocket on the overall front and pin in place. Topstitch around the remaining 3 sides of the pocket, leaving the top open.

SHIRT

1. Fold dart right sides together and sew, using a ⅛˝ seam allowance. (This creates the shoulder seam.)

2. Align a front shirt panel to the front sleeve curve and sew. Repeat for the opposite front side.

3. Align a side of the back shirt panel to the sleeve's curved back edge and sew. Repeat for the opposite side.

4. Fold and press the bottom sleeve edges up ¼˝ and then again ¼˝. Topstitch the sleeve hem.

5. Pin and then sew the arm and side seams.

6. Sew the collar pieces on 3 sides, using a ⅛˝ seam allowance. Refer to Collars (page 66) for finishing the collar.

7. Follow the instructions in Step 4 to hem the bottom of the shirt.

8. Press the front edges of the shirt by turning under ⅛˝ and then again ½˝, and topstitching in place. (I added a small strip of interfacing inside this hem to reinforce the shirt's snap closure.)

9. Topstitch the front edges of the shirt in place. Add snaps, buttons, hook-and-loop tape, or other child-safe closure. (I used 3 snaps.)

SHOES

1. Place a shoe toe on top of a shoe tongue, with the straight edges aligned, and sew along the straight edge with a ⅛˝ seam allowance.

2. Place 2 shoe side pieces wrong sides together and stitch along the inner edge. (I used contrasting thread for detail.) Repeat with the other side of the shoe.

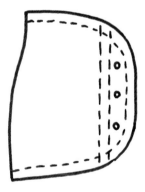

3. Place the 2 shoe side pieces on top of the shoe sole, aligning the curves and matching the top edges with each other. Center a shoe tongue/toe unit on top of the shoe sides, with the seam allowance of the shoe tongue/toe facing up. Pin all 3 layers together. Sew around the entire shoe, leaving the top of the shoe open.

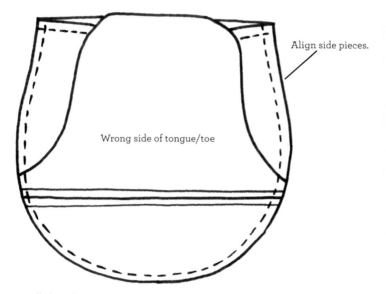

Align side pieces.

Wrong side of tongue/toe

Sew all three layers around outer edge of shoe.

4. Turn the shoe right side out.

5. Use a $^{1}/_{16}$″ craft punch to make 3 holes on each shoe side for laces.

6. With heavy-duty craft thread, narrow twill tape, or doll-sized shoelaces, lace the shoe and tie.

7. Repeat for the other shoe.

Variations

It is quite easy to modify this project. Make this doll a girl, if desired. Try using different materials for hair, such as felt or yarn. Modify the shirt pattern to make a simple jacket for *Small Fry* and include a zipper closure.

how kids can help

Small Fry's shirt is small enough (but not too small) to offer a great opportunity to teach your son or daughter how to hem by hand. Press the hem and hand baste if necessary. Then demonstrate a hemming technique that you feel best suits your little one's abilities.

Sadie, Mae, and Elsie

Finished size: 17˝ tall

This sweet, childlike doll has an irresistible charm! Reminiscent of dozens of mail-order mid-century patterns, the *Sadie, Mae, and Elsie* doll is a modern take on a classic handmade vintage cloth doll. Dressed in a simple wardrobe that can be easily modified to create a collection of clothes, she is certain to appeal to girls of all ages.

Elsie
(See doll variations on pages 61 and 64.)

materials

¾ yard cotton fabric
for each doll body

⅓ yard cotton fabric
for each dress

¼ yard cotton fabric
for bloomers

10″ × 10″ piece cotton
fabric for undershorts

6″ × 8″ piece wool felt
for each pair of shoes

Approximately ⅓ yard ¼″
elastic trim for undershorts
or bloomers

Elastic thread for bloomers

Snaps, buttons, or other
fasteners

Embroidery floss
for facial features

Yarn for hair

Wool stuffing

Optional:
½ yard narrow decorative
trim for undershorts

Sand for weighting
doll body

Instructions

Make the Head and Torso

1. After cutting out all the pieces, use a lightbox or window to transfer all the pattern markings to all the pieces. Make sure to transfer marks to alternate sides of the side pieces (so you have a right and a left side), taking time to carefully draw the sewing lines along the front curves of the face. Those are the lines you will be following when sewing.

2. Sew the darts on the side head pieces. Sew the neck dart a second time for added strength.

notes:

- Use the template patterns on pullout page P2.

- Read all the project instructions before beginning the project.

- Refer to Tools and Techniques (pages 9–13) as needed.

- Trace all pattern pieces onto freezer paper (page 11). (When tracing, match up the front center panel to the back center panel to create one long center head/torso piece.)

- Press freezer-paper templates to the fabric, and cut out the fabric pieces before removing the freezer-paper templates. (When reverse pieces are needed, double the fabric and cut two pattern pieces at a time.)

- Use a short stitch length and sew seams twice!

- Pieces are sewn together with right sides facing, unless otherwise noted.

- The seam allowances are ³⁄₁₆″, unless otherwise noted.

3. Make a few small clips at the necks on both of the side pieces and the center piece to help with pinning and sewing the neck curves.

4. Pin a side piece to the center piece by matching up the dots near the eye line on both pieces. Pin from the eye line and continue to pin at least every ¼˝ down the cheek and also up around the forehead. Match up the front head dart on the side piece to the mark on the center piece.

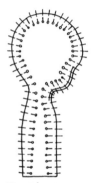

Pin side piece to center piece.

tip If you end up with one piece a bit longer than the other (⅛˝ or more) at the bottom edges of the torso, don't worry. The design of the torso bottom corrects for this. If you pin and end up with substantially more of an overhang (say ½˝), take the pins out and try again.

5. Sew the doll head/torso with the side piece on top and the center piece underneath. Take your time sewing the curves of the face, stopping (in the needle-down position) to pivot as needed. You may have to adjust the fabric a bit every so often so as not to catch extra underneath fabric into the seam.

tip Make sure to sew seams a second time for added durability—the seams can be stressed when the doll is stuffed!

6. Repeat for the opposite side, but leave approximately 2˝ open on the back seam of the doll about midway up for stuffing.

7. Clip or notch curves as needed, and trim the seam allowances along the curves of the face and neck to ⅛˝. Be careful not to cut into the seam allowances.

tip Pinking shears are quite handy when trimming the seam allowances on dolls and toys. Except for the curves of the face and neck of these dolls (where I trim the seam allowances down to ⅛˝ with sharp scissors), I use pinking shears for trimming all other seam allowances. Sometimes an extra notch or two are needed, but often the "notches" created by the pinking shears are enough to provide adequate curves on a small stuffed toy.

8. Sew the darts on the bottom torso piece. Match the 4 darts with the bottom corner seams of the doll torso, pin, and sew all the way around. Clip the bottom seam allowances, as needed.

9. Turn the doll body right side out.

10. Sew around the curved edge of each ear, leaving the straight edge open for turning. Trim and notch the seam allowances, and turn the ears right side out. Turn the straight edge approximately ³/₁₆˝ to the inside and close the ear with a ladder stitch (page 14). Set aside.

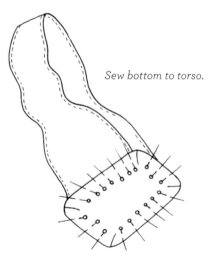

Sew bottom to torso.

Note: Do not sew the ears to the doll until after you have embroidered the features.

Mae
(See doll variations on pages 58 and 64.)

Make the Arms

1. Transfer the pattern markings to the cut arm pieces, taking special care to trace the hands and fingers using an air-erasable or water-soluble marker.

2. Pin the 2 arm pieces together and use the marks as a guide to sew around the arm. Make sure to leave an opening as designated on the pattern piece.

tip Use the needle-down position on the sewing machine to make sewing fingers easier. Sew slowly, using a short stitch length, and with the needle down, stop and pivot the fabric around the curves.

3. Trim the seam allowances using pinking shears, with the exception of the hand and fingers.

4. Use sharp scissors to trim the hand and finger seam allowances down to ⅛˝.

5. Clip notches and curves where needed. Be careful not to cut through the seam allowances.

6. Turn the arm right side out.

7. Repeat to make the other arm.

Make the Legs

1. Pin 2 leg pieces together and sew the side seams, leaving the top and bottom of the leg open.

2. Baste the sole of the foot to the bottom of the leg and sew. (Hand basting is strongly recommended.)

3. Trim and clip the seam allowances, and turn right side out.

4. Repeat for the other leg. Be sure to sew a right and a left leg by reversing the placement of the sole of the foot.

Stuff the Doll

Keep in mind that stuffing these dolls is, and should be, a process—so stuff slowly. If you plan to weight the doll with a small, securely sewn bag of sand (see Tip, page 13), insert it while stuffing and place it at the bottom of the torso.

1. Refer to Stuffing and Finishing (page 13) for general tips about stuffing. Start by stuffing the doll's head. Mist the head with water and gently finger-press the front face seams toward the side pieces (continue to gently finger press these seams from time to time while stuffing the head). Use small amounts of wool and pack layer by layer. Midway through the stuffing process, you may think the head looks rather distorted, but continue to pack the stuffing and move it around to fill gaps. The head will continue to change shape and fill out.

2. Place a small sand bag inside the bottom of the torso (*optional*), and then start to stuff the torso. Continue stuffing until the head and torso are very firm. When you think you are finished stuffing—stuff some more! Turn in the seam allowance on the back torso opening, and sew closed using a ladder stitch.

3. Begin stuffing the arms and legs. Use a stuffing tool (I prefer a pair of hemostats) to gently pack small wads of wool stuffing into the fingers, then the hands, then the arms; the feet, then the legs. Stuff both arms and legs more lightly at the tops. This will allow more freedom of movement and will help when the doll is sitting.

4. Turn in the seam allowances of the openings in the arms and legs, and sew them closed using a ladder stitch.

Make the Face and Hair

Refer to All About Faces and Hair (pages 17–42) and embroider a face. Then use a ladder stitch to sew on the ears over the knots. Sew the straight edge of the ear to the head and continue to sew the underside of the ear to the head, hiding all embroidery work in the process. Add a yarn hairstyle of your choosing.

Assemble the Doll

1. Thread a strong needle with an arm's length of upholstery or heavy button thread that matches the color of the doll body.

2. Use a ladder stitch to sew the tops of the arms slightly below the bottom of the neck dart.

3. Take stitches between the inner shoulders of the arms and the doll's torso. Lift the arms and use the ladder stitch to also secure the arms to the body from underneath to assure that each arm is sewn on securely on both the top and the bottom. Figure A.

4. Use a ladder stitch to sew the legs to the bottom of the doll torso. I like to sew them a little closer to the front seam, which allows the doll to sit a bit more easily. Figure B.

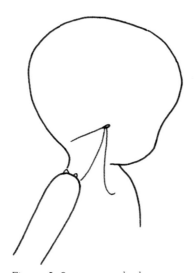

Figure A. Sew arms to body.

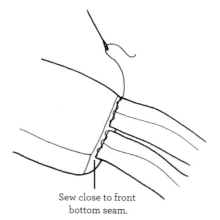

Sew close to front
bottom seam.

Figure B. Sew legs to body.

Sadie
(See doll variations on pages 58 and 61.)

Make the Clothing

The dress pattern is extremely simple and can be easily modified into a tunic-style shirt or short dress (as for Elsie) or a long-sleeved dress (as for Sadie). The neckline can be finished with a simple Peter Pan collar, bias trim, or decorative lace for an easy finish.

DRESS

1. Pin the front edge of the sleeve to the front sleeve seam of the dress. Sew using a $3/16''$ seam allowance. Repeat for the other side. Figure A.

2. Pin the back edge of the sleeve to the back sleeve seam of the dress and sew. Repeat for the other side. Figure B.

3. For short sleeves, press under a small $1/4''$–$3/16''$ hem on the sleeve edges and edgestitch or apply bias tape. For long sleeves, slightly gather the bottom of the sleeve, pin the edge to the cuff, and sew. Press the other edge of the cuff $1/8''$ inward and then again $5/8''$, and topstitch down.

4. Pin the front and back of the dress together at the sides and sew the sleeve and side seam on both sides. Figure C.

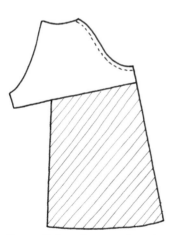
Figure A. Sew sleeve to dress front.

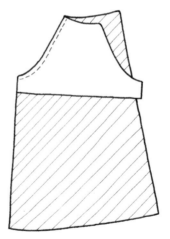
Figure B. Sew sleeve to dress back.

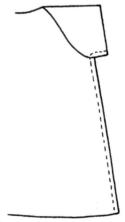
Figure C. Sew dress sides.

5. For a faux button placket, take a 2″ × 3″ piece of fabric, fold, and then sew along the side and bottom raw edges, leaving the top edge open. Clip the corners and turn it right side out. Press. Topstitch the placket in place and sew on buttons.

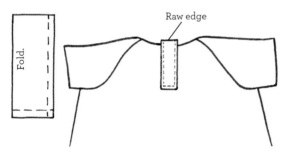

6. Finish the raw edge of the neck with either bias tape, a decorative trim, a ⅛″ hem, or a collar.

7. Finish the bottom edge of the dress with bias tape; or fold under and press the bottom dress edge ¼″ and again ½″ toward the inside, and then use a blind stitch (page 14) to hem the dress.

8. Fold under and press the raw back edge of the dress ¼″ and then again ½″. Topstitch down.

9. Add snaps or buttons to the back of the dress. (I used 3 snaps.)

collars

To add a collar to a dress or shirt, refer to the recommended seam allowance and sew the collar pieces. Clip the curves and corners, as needed, and turn the collar pieces right side out. For a girl's dress, center the collar pieces near the center front of the dress and baste in place. For a boy's shirt, center the collar at the back of the shirt and pin or baste. Make bias tape (page 13) from the dress or shirt fabric or use packaged bias tape. Apply the bias tape around the raw neck edge and sew. Press the bias tape toward the inside of the dress or shirt and topstitch under the collar to secure the folded neck edge in place.

Baste collar.   *Apply bias tape around neck opening.*   *Fold bias tape under neck opening and topstitch.*

UNDERSHORTS

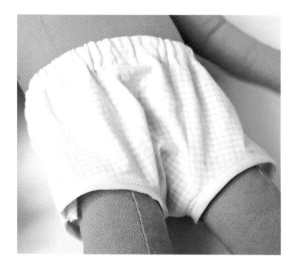

2. Fold on the dashed crotch line and align the side seams. Pin, and then sew using a ³/₁₆˝ seam allowance.

3. Finish the side seams or use pinking shears to trim. Turn the undershorts right side out.

4. Fold and press the top raw edge of the waist ⅛˝ to the inside, and turn and press again ½˝.

5. Edgestitch to create a casing, leaving a 1˝ opening near the back seam.

6. Thread elastic through the waistband casing, taking care not to twist the elastic. Overlap the ends of the elastic and use a safety pin to secure them.

7. Test the undershorts on the doll and adjust as necessary.

8. Sew the overlapped ends securely by hand or machine.

9. Fit the elastic inside the casing and sew the opening closed.

1. Press the undershorts piece flat and add trim, lace, or bias tape to leg curves/holes.

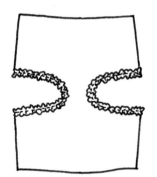

Apply trim to undershorts.

ELSIE'S BLOOMER PANTS

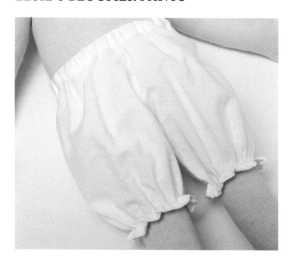

1. Place the 2 leg seams of a bloomer pants piece right sides together and sew. Repeat for the other piece. Finish the seam allowances.

Sew bloomer leg seam.

2. Turn a leg right side out and place inside the other leg (right sides facing), aligning the leg seams. Pin and then sew the front and back seam as a single long seam.

3. Fold and press the edge of each leg opening ¼˝ to the wrong side and then another ¼˝ to the wrong side, and edgestitch in place.

4. With elastic thread wound in the bobbin of your sewing machine, sew around each leg opening ¼˝ above edge stitching. The elastic thread will gather the fabric as you sew.

5. Turn the bloomers right side out and follow Undershorts, Steps 4–9 (page 67), for making the waist casing.

SHOES

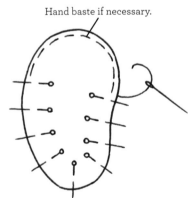

This pattern was designed to make a doll that can wear shoes sized for an 18˝ doll; however, it is quite simple to make a pair of shoes out of wool felt.

1. Take the U-shaped shoe piece and fold it, aligning the 2 short edges.

Sew upper shoe.

2. Sew by machine or by hand with a ⅛˝ seam allowance.

3. Pin or baste the top part of the shoe to the sole, starting from the center of the toe and going around to the heel, and then starting again at the toe and going around the other side to the heel.

Hand baste if necessary.

Pin upper shoe to sole.

4. Sew by machine or by hand, with a ⅛˝ seam allowance.

5. Turn the shoe right side out and use your finger to gently press the seam to create a more rounded shoe. Repeat for the other shoe. Make sure to reverse the placement of the sole to create a right and a left shoe.

Variations

The following four dolls are variations of this type of doll: The Cone Puppet (pages 92–96) and Little Red (pages 77–81) have heads that are similar in construction to these dolls. Goldilocks (pages 82–91) has a similar head and torso. The Marionettes (pages 70–76) are similar but smaller.

For this particular doll pattern, however, there are a few subtle changes that you can make.

- The arms can be jointed with buttons.

- The hair can be crocheted as a wig.

- The doll can be made as a boy (see Jack marionette, pages 41 and 75, for ideas).

- The clothes patterns are basic and can be altered to make a wardrobe of doll clothes. For example, the dress pattern can be lengthened to make a nightgown and the shoes can be made as a pair of slippers (add little bunny ears!).

- Experiment with different facial expressions and hairstyles to create a doll all your own!

how kids can help

It generally takes me up to four hours to stuff each one of these dolls! It can be time-consuming, but luckily this is a process with which my kids always like to help, particularly my youngest. She likes to tear off bits of wool stuffing and hand them to me, sometimes even stuffing bits of wool herself. I move the stuffing around and my daughter gets the next bit of wool ready. A perfect assembly line!

For children with basic sewing skills, the dress, under-shorts, and bloomers are simple enough patterns for kids to adapt and design doll clothes on their own, or with a bit of adult assistance.

Jack and Jill Marionettes

Finished size: 12˝ tall (excluding marionette controls)

M arionettes capture the imagination of children and adults alike. Be it watching a puppet dance or controlling the strings, people have a natural fascination with manipulating these puppets and watching them move. Jack and Jill are smaller than, but similar to Sadie, Mae, and Elsie. The simple marionette design, which is perfect for kids, helps bring this delightful duo to life.

materials

½ yard cotton fabric (will make 2 doll bodies)

¼ yard cotton fabric for Jack's shirt

¼ yard cotton fabric for Jill's dress

8˝ × 10˝ piece cotton fabric for Jack's shorts or Jill's undershorts

6˝ × 6˝ piece wool felt for each pair of shoes

8˝ × 9˝ scrap felted wool for Jill's bolero

Approximately ¼ yard ¼˝ elastic for Jack's shorts or Jill's undershorts

4 doll-sized buttons for Jack's shirt

Embroidery floss for facial features

Yarn for hair

Wool stuffing

Wool felt scrap for lining torso bottom

4 buttons (⅜˝) for each marionette—2 for hands, 2 for knees

Sand or other material for weighting doll bodies

Black upholstery thread for marionette strings

For each marionette control:

5 wooden beads (8mm)

¾˝ × ¾˝ piece of wood 10˝ long

¼˝ × 1½˝ piece of wood 8˝ long

2 eye screws (¼˝–⅜˝)

2 small screws

Instructions

Make the Head and Torso

1. Refer to Steps 1–10 in Make the Head and Torso of *Sadie, Mae, and Elsie* (pages 59 and 60) for instructions on sewing the head and torso pieces.

2. Refer to Stuffing and Finishing (page 13) for general tips about stuffing. Stuff the head firmly, leaving the torso unstuffed. Mark the center top of the head (this spot can vary slightly depending on how a doll was sewn and stuffed).

notes:

- *Use the template patterns on pages 138–142.*

- *Read all the project instructions before beginning the project.*

- *Refer to Tools and Techniques (pages 9–13) as needed.*

- *Trace all pattern pieces onto freezer paper (page 11). When tracing, match up the front center panel to the back center panel to create a long center head/torso piece.*

- *Press freezer-paper templates to the fabric and cut out the fabric pieces before removing the freezer-paper templates.*

- *Pieces are sewn together with right sides facing, unless otherwise noted.*

- *Use a short stitch length, and sew seams twice for added durability.*

- *The seam allowances are ³⁄₁₆˝, unless otherwise noted.*

3. Place a small scrap of wool felt inside the bottom of the doll torso for added strength.

4. Thread a long doll needle with a long (about 40˝) piece of black upholstery thread and knot the tail of the thread. Bring the needle into the doll body through the opening in the doll's back torso seam and exit at the center bottom of the doll.

5. Take 2–3 small stitches here (going back into the doll and out) to secure the thread to the center bottom.

6. Repeat Steps 4 and 5, and secure a second string to the center bottom of the doll's torso.

7. Thread the first string on a long doll needle and go back into the doll's bottom center. Bring the needle and thread all the way up the inside of the doll, through the center of the neck and head, and out at the center top of the doll's head.

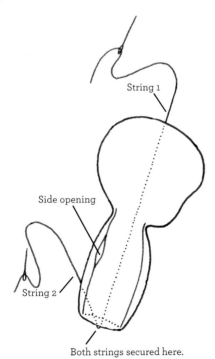

String head and torso.

8. Unthread the doll needle and place a few pins at the top of the head. Wind the excess thread around these pins several times to keep it out of the way.

9. Rethread the second string on a long needle, bring it back through the bottom center, and exit 1˝ above the back seam, centered between the 2 back side seams.

10. Use a bit of sand to weight the bottom of the doll body.

tip The safest method for weighting a doll or toy with sand is to sew a small pouch and fill it with sand. Marionettes aren't handled in quite the same way as a traditional rag doll, so I just add the sand directly into the torso, hands, and arms. This seems to work well. Be sure that all seams are sewn twice with a short stitch length.

11. Continue to stuff the rest of the torso until firm, moving the stuffing around the 2 threads inside the doll torso.

12. Close the opening with a ladder stitch (page 14).

13. Wrap the second string hanging from the lower back of the torso around the doll's body to keep it out of the way until String the Marionette (page 76).

Make the Arms

1. Transfer the pattern markings to an arm piece for each arm, including the sewing lines for the hands.

2. Pin 2 arm pieces together and sew, leaving the top of the arm open for stuffing.

3. Clip and notch the curves as needed, trim seam allowances, and turn the arm right side out.

4. Place a small amount of wool stuffing in the hand up to the beginning of the thumb.

5. Secure the end of a long (40˝) piece of black upholstery thread through a small button (⅜˝ or smaller) for puppet string.

6. Thread the opposite end of the thread through a doll needle and take the needle into the doll's arm. Bring the doll needle and thread out of the arm near the thumb, above the inner palm of the hand, and pull the button into place inside the hand.

7. Secure the button inside the hand with a bit more wool and add a bit of sand to lightly weight the arm.

8. Continue to stuff the rest of the arm up to the elbow area (approximately halfway up the arm).

9. Hand stitch across the elbow joint (the seams should be aligned along the center of the arm).

10. Lightly stuff the upper arm.

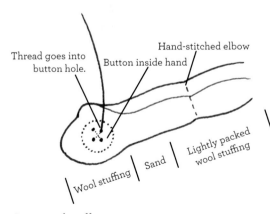

String and stuff arm.

11. Turn under the raw edge of the arm, aligning the seams at the center.

12. Use a ladder stitch to sew the arm securely to the doll body near the shoulder area.

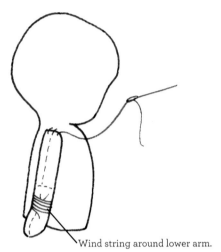

Wind string around lower arm.

Sew arm to torso.

13. Wrap the excess string around the lower arm to keep it out of the way until you are ready to string the marionette to the control. Repeat for the other arm.

Make the Legs

Refer to Make the Legs of *Sadie, Mae, and Elsie* (page 62) to sew the marionettes' legs.

1. Turn the legs right side out and add a small amount of wool stuffing to line the bottom of the foot.

2. Weight the foot with sand up to 1˝ up from the bottom of the leg. Add wool stuffing up to the knee.

3. Take a long (40˝) piece of black upholstery thread and secure the end through a small (⅜˝ or smaller) button for puppet string.

4. Thread the opposite end of the thread through a doll needle. Bring the needle, thread, and button into the leg, and exit at the back of the knee (right near the center back seam). Take a stitch back into the leg, *through* the button, exiting at the front of the knee to secure the button inside the leg.

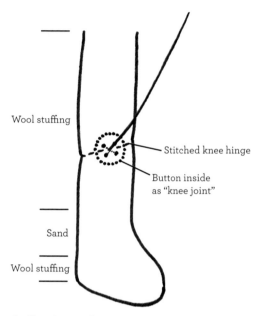

Stuff and string leg.

5. Use thread that matches the doll body to take a few small stitches on either side of the button to finish off the knee hinge.

6. Stuff the top part of the leg lightly with wool.

7. Turn under the raw edges of the leg and sew the leg securely to the doll body near the front bottom seam, using a ladder stitch. (Make sure, once again, that the leg seams are aligned in the center.)

8. Wrap excess upholstery thread around the bottom part of the leg to keep it out of the way.

9. Repeat for the other leg.

Make the Faces and Hair

1. Refer to All About Faces and Hair (pages 16–24) and embroider the facial features using the face template patterns provided.

2. Use a ladder stitch to sew the ears to the head (page 60). The ears will cover the tack stitches for the facial features.

3. Add a yarn wig or embroidered hairstyle (pages 37–41).

Make the Clothes

The clothes patterns included are very basic designs and easy to alter. Keep in mind that marionette clothes should allow for movement, so avoid stiff, heavy materials.

Marionettes cannot have their clothes changed because of the strings; therefore you can sew each piece firmly to the marionette as you go along. You should be able to easily design and customize your own marionette's clothing with little effort and a bit of creativity.

JILL'S DRESS

1. Place the bodice front and a bodice back together and sew along the shoulder seam. Repeat for the other side.

2. Fold and press a ⅛˝ hem around the arm opening and edgestitch it in place. Add trim during this step if desired.

3. Pin the front and back of the bodice pieces, right sides together, and sew the side seams. Press the side seams open.

4. Fold the back edges of the dress opening ¼˝ toward the inside on each side; press and sew.

5. Turn under the neck opening ⅛˝, press, and sew.

6. Cut a skirt piece 4⅛″ × 20″. Pin the short edges of the skirt together and sew. Press the seam open.

7. Fold under the bottom edge of the skirt ⅛″ and then another ¼″, and topstitch for the hem.

8. Overlap the back bodice pieces by ¼″ and hand baste, if necessary. Gather the top edge of the skirt and fit it to the dress bodice, aligning the skirt seam with the back of the bodice.

9. Sew the skirt to the dress bodice.

10. The back of the dress can be sewn directly to the doll's torso. Buttons can be added for a decorative accent, if desired.

JILL'S BOLERO

1. Fold along the dotted shoulder line and then pin the bolero sleeves and sides together.

2. Sew the arm and side seams, using a ⅛″ seam allowance. Turn the bolero right side out.

Note: If you are using a material that will fray, simply turn under the raw outer edges, add a decorative trim, or both.

JACK'S SHIRT

Follow Steps 1–8 for Shirt in *Small Fry* (pages 55 and 56) for basic instructions on making the shirt. Press and sew the front edges of the shirt by turning under the edge ¼″ and then another ¼″. Add 4 doll-sized buttons as a decorative accent.

JACK'S SHORTS AND JILL'S UNDERSHORTS

Follow Steps 1–3 of Elsie's Bloomer Pants in *Sadie, Mae, and Elsie* (pages 67 and 68) for instructions on making the shorts. Press the waist edge under ³⁄₁₆″ and again ³⁄₁₆″ to create the casing for the waistband. Do not gather the legs of the shorts. Hem the boy's shorts and add bias tape or other decorative trim to the girl's undershorts.

SHOES

Follow the steps in Shoes from *Sadie, Mae, and Elsie* (page 68) for instructions on making felt shoes.

Make a Simple Marionette Control

A simple marionette control can be made using two pieces of wood. For the controls used here, I used a ¾″ × ¾″ piece of wood 10″ long and a ¼″ × 1½″ piece of wood 8″ long. I have the arms, legs, and bottom strung through the control to beads so that there is even more movement, making it easy for kids to manipulate. A simple tug of a bead causes a hand to wave hello.

1. Place the 2 pieces of wood in a T formation, with the wider piece of wood at the top of the T. Secure the wood from the top with 2 screws.

2. Add an eye screw, according to the diagram (page 76), on the underside of the lower stick, 2⅜″ from the front edge. A second eye screw can be added to the top of the control to hang the control on a stand (*optional*). See Resources (page 160) for marionette stands.

3. Drill small holes for the puppet strings, according to the diagram (page 76). Holes A (for arm strings) are ½″ from the outer edges and holes L (for leg strings) are 1½″ inside of A. The bottom string hole is ½″ from the back edge of the control. (Alternatively, the strings can be securely tied around the marionette control if no drill is available.)

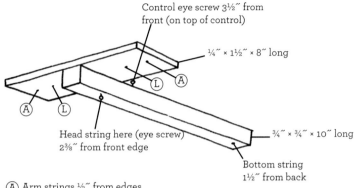

Control eye screw 3½˝ from front (on top of control)

¼˝ × 1½˝ × 8˝ long

Ⓛ Ⓐ

Ⓐ Ⓛ

Head string here (eye screw) 2⅜˝ from front edge

¾˝ × ¾˝ × 10˝ long

Bottom string 1½˝ from back

Ⓐ Arm strings ½˝ from edges

Ⓛ Leg strings 1½˝ from Ⓐ

Marionette control

String the Marionette

For the average marionette, the head string measures 30˝ to the control. For a young child to use, however, this measurement can be as small as 14˝.

1. Fasten the head string to the underside eye screw so that the puppet stands upright. Tie using a secure knot or two.

2. Use a needle to thread the back/bottom string through the doll's clothing. Test to make sure the string allows for adequate movement. Thread this string through the hole at the back edge of the control and securely knot it to a bead. The bead should sit atop the marionette control.

3. Thread the arm strings through their respective holes (A) and secure them to beads. The arms should lie at the marionette's side and the strings should look taut.

4. Thread the knee strings through their respective holes (L) and secure them to beads. The legs should be straight and should lift easily at the knee as you rotate the controls.

5. Trim the excess strings.

Variations

A clown, wizard, witch, or little Pinocchio—the possibilities for the cast of marionette characters are endless! Or simply use the pattern to make a smaller 12˝ doll.

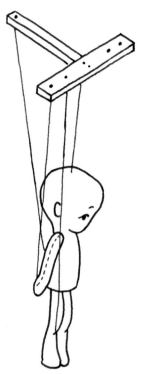

String puppet.

how kids can help

Marionettes can be tricky to string unless you have a marionette stand (see Resources, page 160). Involve your children and have them hold the marionette control and test how it works. Besides, this is the fun part—watching the puppet come to life!

Little Red Riding Hood Puppet Set

Finished size: 12˝ tall

This charming Little Red puppet set draws on both the contoured-head construction of *Sadie, Mae, and Elsie* and the design of *Topsy-Turvy Goldilocks and the Three Bears*. With Little Red on one hand and Grandma and the wolf on the other, your child will have an instant puppet show!

½ yard cotton fabric for both puppet heads and hands

½ yard cotton or cotton-linen fabric for Little Red's body/dress and hooded cape lining

½ yard cotton or cotton-linen fabric for Grandma's body/dress and nightcap

¼ yard fabric for Little Red's hooded cape (I used boiled wool)

8″ × 11″ piece of wool felt for wolf's face and hands

2 different yarns for Little Red's and Grandma's hair

Stuffing

Embroidery floss for features

Wool felt scraps for wolf's face

Wool felt scraps for mushroom appliqué

Approximately 15″ of elastic ¼″ wide for nightcap

¾″ button for cape

2½″ piece of elastic trim or cording for button loop

Optional:
1¼ yards lace for nightcap

1¼ yards trim for cape

Instructions

Make the Puppet Heads

Follow the instructions in *Sadie, Mae, and Elsie* (pages 59 and 60) for sewing the puppet heads. Keep in mind that there is no torso or "bottom" piece.

LITTLE RED

1. Refer to Stuffing and Finishing (page 13) for general tips about stuffing. Stuff the puppet head. Use your fingers to push the wool and create a space to allow fingers to control the move-ment of the puppet head. Use a stuffing tool to help create this space, if necessary.

notes:

- Use the template patterns on pages 143–146, and pullout page P4.

- Read all the project instructions before beginning the project.

- Refer to Tools and Techniques (pages 9–13) as needed.

- Trace all pattern pieces onto freezer paper (page 11).

- Press freezer-paper templates to the fabric, and cut out the fabric pieces before removing the freezer-paper templates.

- Pieces are sewn together with right sides facing, unless otherwise noted.

- Use a short stitch length.

- The seam allowances are $3/16$″, unless otherwise noted.

2. Use the provided face template pattern or your own design. Refer to All About Faces and Hair (pages 17–42) and embroider Little Red's face, sew on her ears, and securely sew her hairstyle in place.

3. Pin 2 pieces of the puppet head lining together and sew, leaving the straight edge open. Fold and press a small hem on the puppet head lining piece.

4. Finger-press the edges of the puppet head toward the inside.

5. Insert the puppet head lining inside the puppet head and whipstitch (page 14) it in place around the edges.

GRANDMA AND THE WOLF

Note: Use a ⅛″ seam allowance for sewing the wolf's face and ears.

1. Refer to Step 1 of Little Red Riding Hood (page 78) to stuff and prepare the Grandma puppet head, leaving space for fingers to control.

2. Use the provided face template pattern or design your own. Refer to All About Faces and Hair (pages 16–24) and embroider Grandma's facial features. Do not add her hair yet.

3. Pin and sew 2 wolf side head pieces together from the nose down to the neckline.

4. Pin the head gusset in place and sew. Turn the wolf's face right side out.

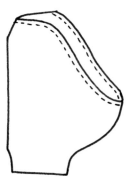

5. Pin 2 wolf ear pieces together and sew, leaving the bottom edge open. Clip the corners and turn the ear right side out. Repeat for the other ear.

6. Sew the wolf's face to the back of Grandma's head using a whipstitch, taking care to stuff the wolf's face as you go.

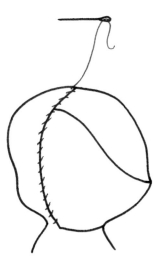

Attach wolf's face to Grandma's head.

7. To attach the ears, make small cuts near the top of the wolf's head, approximately ¾″ from the back edge of the felt. Insert the bottom edges of the ears and whipstitch the ears securely in place.

8. Refer to Little Red, Steps 3–5 (page 79), to attach the head lining.

9. Refer to All About Faces and Hair (pages 25–34) and give Grandma some curls out of gray yarn.

10. Appliqué the wolf's features out of wool felt.

Make the Puppet Bodies

1. Pin the puppet hands to the front and back puppet bodies/dresses at the sleeve edges and sew. Sew Grandma's hands to the front of Grandma's body and the wolf's hands to the back of Grandma's body.

2. Pin Little Red's body front to body back and sew from the neck edge all the way around to the corresponding bottom edge (leaving the neck edge open, as designated on the pattern). Repeat for other side. Do the same for Grandma's body.

3. Fold ¼˝ under on the bottom edge and then fold another ½˝ under to hem Little Red's body/dress. You may do the same for Grandma or add a ruffle. If you choose to add a ruffle, cut a strip 1½˝ × 30˝. Sew the short ends together. Make a narrow hem on a long edge of the strip and sew gathering stitches on the other edge.

Gather the strip, pin to the bottom edge of the body/dress, and sew together.

4. Press a ¼˝ hem on the neck edges of the puppet bodies toward the inside.

Make Little Red's Hooded Cape

1. Pin and sew the darts in the cape and hood.

2. Pin 2 hood pieces together and sew along the top and back of the hood.

3. Align the hood darts to the cape darts and sew the hood to the cape around the neck edge.

4. Repeat Steps 1–3 for the hood and cape lining.

5. Pin the ends of a 2½˝ piece of elastic trim or cording together and baste in place at the neck edge, matching the ends with the raw edges of the cape. (I used a ¼˝ × 2½˝ strip of boiled wool.) Pin the lining and cape together, adding trim during this step if desired. Sew, leaving a 2˝ opening on the bottom back edge of the cape, as designated on the pattern, to turn the cape right side out.

Note: The length of the button loop depends on the size of the button you use. Be sure to test it on the button before stitching the loop onto the cape.

Turn through opening on back bottom edge of cape.

Sew hooded cape and lining.

6. Trim the seam allowances and turn through the opening in the back.

7. Close the opening with a ladder stitch (page 14).

Make Grandma and Wolf Nightcap

1. Pin the outer nightcap to the inner nightcap brim, adding lace or trim if desired. Sew around the outer edge of the nightcap and clip seam allowances.

2. Turn the nightcap right side out and press.

3. Sew approximately ⅝˝ from the inside edge of the inner nightcap brim. Sew again, ⅛˝ from the edge, to create a casing. Make sure to leave a 1˝ opening.

4. Insert ¼˝ elastic. Trim and fit to the Grandma/wolf head. Secure the elastic ends and close the opening.

Finish the Puppets

1. Appliqué the mushroom near the bottom edge of Little Red's dress.

2. Sew a button to the cape.

3. Securely sew the puppet bodies to the heads at the neckline.

4. Place the nightcap on the Grandma/wolf head and fasten Little Red's cape in place.

Note: You can use recycled glass or plastic water bottles as stands. Or for a more child-friendly stand, make a dowel-and-wood base.

how kids can help

The appliquéd mushroom on the front of Little Red's dress is a perfect opportunity to involve little hands. Both of my older daughters have appliquéd similar felt shapes to hand-made doll dresses over the years. If working with a young child or a child new to sewing, make holes prior to sewing using a ¹/₁₆˝ craft punch for your child to follow, as shown.

Variations

The basic head and simple body construction lend themselves to so many possibilities! Brainstorm with your children or search through their favorite picture books for added inspiration.

Topsy-Turvy Goldilocks and the Three Bears

Finished size: 18˝ tall

R eferred to as a "topsy-turvy," "upside down," or "turn-about" doll, Goldilocks and the Three Bears makes an entertaining addition when reciting the beloved nursery tale for the seventh time in a row! Make no mistake, this is a time-intensive project, but when you are done you will have created a truly classic heirloom toy.

See bears on pages 85 and 88.

⅔ yard cotton fabric for Goldilocks' body

⅔ yard cotton fabric for Goldilocks' dress

¼ yard cotton fabric for the bears' torso

⅓ yard cotton fabric for Mama's and Papa's skirts

⅓ yard corduroy for Papa's pants

⅓ yard fabric for Mama's apron

⅓ yard fabric for Goldilocks' apron

18″ × 18″ piece brown wool felt for bear heads, bear paws, and Baby Bear

6″ × 8″ scrap felted wool for Papa's vest

2 buttons for Papa's vest

24″ piece of double-fold bias tape to coordinate with Mama's apron (or make your own bias tape)

Yarn for Goldilocks' hair

Embroidery floss for facial features

Black wool felt scraps for bear features

Elastic thread

Stuffing

Optional:
12″ piece of medium rickrack or trim for Goldilocks' apron

12″ piece each of narrow rickrack or trim for Goldilocks' and Mama's collars

Instructions

Make Goldilocks' Head, Torso, and Arms

1. Refer to *Sadie, Mae, and Elsie* (pages 59–62) for instructions on how to sew the head and torso pieces together as well as how to make the ears and arms. After sewing the arm and stuffing it, fold ½″ of the top edge toward the inside and close the opening using a ladder stitch (page 14).

2. Refer to Stuffing and Finishing (page 13) for general tips about stuffing.

notes:

- Use the template patterns on pages 147–151 and pullout page P3.

- Read all the project instructions before beginning the project.

- Refer to Tools and Techniques (pages 9–13) as needed.

- Trace all pattern pieces onto freezer paper (page 11).

- Press freezer-paper templates to the fabric, and cut out the fabric pieces before removing the freezer-paper templates.

- Pieces are sewn together with right sides facing, unless otherwise noted.

- Use a short stitch length.

- The seam allowances are ³⁄₁₆″, unless otherwise noted. For Goldilocks' dress and Mama's and Papa's skirts, the seam allowances are ¼″.

Note: Goldilocks' and the bears' torsos are sewn separately and then attached while stuffing the bears' torso.

Stuff the head and torso firmly and close the side opening with a ladder stitch (page 14).

3. Refer to All About Faces and Hair (pages 17–42) for instructions on embroidering Goldilocks' facial features and adding the hair. Sew on the ears after finishing the face, but prior to adding the hair.

Make the Bears' Head

The bears' head features Mama Bear on one side and Papa Bear on the other. The heads are each sewn in a similar manner and then sewn together to make a two-sided head.

1. Align and pin 2 bear head sides, and sew from the nose to the neck. Repeat for the remaining bear head sides.

Bear head

2. Align and pin a bear head gusset in place between the head sides, and sew. Repeat for the remaining bear head.

Bear head gusset

3. Pin 2 bear ear pieces together and sew. Turn the ear right side out. Repeat for the remaining 2 ear pieces.

4. Turn a bear face right side out. Hand baste the ears in place at the top of the head, right sides facing, centering the ears over the front seams.

Hand baste bear ears.

5. Pin the 2 bear faces, right sides together, and sew around the face edges from one side of the neck to the remaining side. Leave the neck open. Turn the head right side out.

Make the Bears' Torso

1. Add decorative trim to Mama's collar if desired and sew around the collar, as shown. Fold and stitch an end of each piece of Papa's collar as shown.

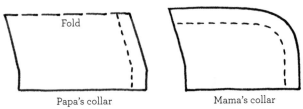

Papa's collar   Mama's collar

Sew collars.

Topsy-Turvy Goldilocks and the Three Bears

2. Open out Mama's collar and unfold Papa's collar. Refer to the pattern and pin together an end of Mama's collar to an end of Papa's collar, right sides facing, and sew along the straight edge. Clip seam allowances and turn the collar piece right side out. Repeat with the 2 other collar pieces.

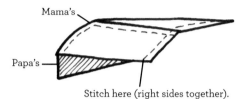

Mama's

Papa's

Stitch here (right sides together).

Sew collars together.

3. Sew 2 bear torso pieces together along the front seam. Repeat for the remaining torso pieces.

4. Pin the bear torso units from Step 3 together and sew the side seams, leaving the top and bottom edges open.

5. Turn the bears' torso right side out and align the raw edges of the collars in place with the neck opening. Match up the collar seams with the side and front seams and sew them in place. Papa's collar pieces should meet at a torso front and Mama's should meet at the other front.

6. Turn the torso inside out and place the 2-sided bear head, right side out and upside down, inside the bears' torso. Pin in place at the neckline, using the side and center seams to align the head and torso. Sew the head to the torso and then turn right side out.

7. Align the straight edge of a bear paw with the bottom edge of a bear sleeve and sew. Press the seam toward the sleeve and topstitch on the reverse side. Repeat for the remaining paws and sleeves to make the bears' arms.

8. Pin 2 bear arms together and sew, leaving the top edge of the bear arm open.

9. Notch the seam allowances and turn the arm right side out. Stuff the arm, leaving the upper portion of the arm more lightly stuffed.

10. Turn in the raw edges of the arm ¼˝ toward the inside, align the seams in the center of the arm, and close with a ladder stitch.

11. Repeat Steps 8–10 for the remaining arm. Set the arms aside.

Attach the Torsos

1. Fold and press the lower edge of the bears' torso inward by approximately ⅜˝.

2. Stuff the bears' head and the upper part of their torso firmly. Lightly stuff the middle part of the torso.

3. Fit the lower edge of the bears' torso over the bottom of Goldilocks' torso and pin in place. Align the front seam of the bears' torso with the center of Goldilocks' front. Align the bears' side seams with the centers of Goldilocks' sides.

4. Sew once around with upholstery thread and a long ladder stitch.

5. Sew around the torsos again and use a stuffing tool to insert stuffing into the bears' torso through the long stitches.

6. Sew around again, and as the stuffing becomes firmer, make the stitches smaller until the bears' torso is firmly stuffed and securely sewn to Goldilocks' torso.

7. Use a ladder stitch to attach the bears' and Goldilocks' arms to the torsos.

Make the Clothing

The clothing is sewn separately and then attached at the bottom hems. Note that both Goldilocks' dress and the bears' skirts use ¼˝ seam allowances.

GOLDILOCKS' DRESS

1. Align and pin a dress bodice back at the shoulder to the dress bodice front, right sides facing, and sew. Repeat for the other side.

2. Sew the sleeves to the dress bodice, gathering slightly at the shoulder.

3. Hem each sleeve by turning under ¼˝ of the lower edge and topstitching.

4. Pin and then sew the sleeve and side bodice seams.

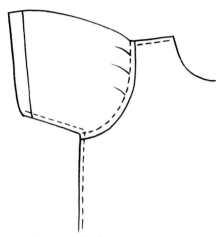

Sew sleeve and bodice seam.

5. Insert a needle and elastic thread into the sleeve hem (through the stitching on the inside). Tighten the thread and secure with a knot.

6. Refer to Collars (page 66). Pin and then sew 2 collar pieces together along the outer curved edge, adding trim if desired. Repeat for the remaining collar pieces. Clip the seam allowances, turn right side out, and press.

7. Sew the collar to the dress neck edge. Make and apply bias tape (page 13) to finish the edge of the neck, as described in *Sadie, Mae, and Elsie* (page 66).

8. Fold and press a ¼˝ hem on the back edges of the bodice pieces.

9. Cut an 11˝ × 36½˝ piece for the skirt. Pin the 2 short edges of the skirt piece together and sew, using a ¼˝ seam allowance. *Leave the top 4˝ of the seam open.*

10. With the skirt inside out, press the seam allowance open, including the unsewn portion.

11. Gather the top edge of the skirt and fit it to the dress bodice, aligning the bodice and skirt back openings. Unfold the pressed hems on both the back bodice pieces and the skirt. Pin and then sew the skirt to the bodice.

12. Refold the pressed hems of the back bodice pieces and skirt opening, and edgestitch.

MAMA AND PAPA BEAR'S SKIRTS

1. Cut an 11″ × 18½″ piece for each bear's skirt. Pin Mama's skirt to Papa's skirt material at both shorter sides and sew, using a ¼″ seam allowance.

2. Align and pin Mama's skirt and Papa's skirt to the bottom edge of Goldilocks' dress. If you are using different fabric for Mama and Papa, make sure that the skirts correspond with the correct side of Goldilocks' dress and will match up with the Mama or Papa side of the bears' torso (based on their collar design).

3. Sew together the bottom edges of the skirts and dress, and turn right side out.

Sew bottom edge of Goldilocks' dress to bottom edges of Mama's/Papa's skirt.

Mama/Papa Bear's skirt (right sides facing) Sew to Goldilocks' dress bottom edge.

4. Dress Goldilocks and secure the dress to her body by sewing buttons to the back of the dress bodice. Her dress will not be removable, so you can also just stitch the dress to her body if desired. Hand sew the back of the skirt opening closed (*optional*).

5. Turn the doll upside down and secure the upper edge of the bears' skirt to their waists by gathering and hand sewing to the bears' torso. Align the seams of the skirt to the torso side seams.

Secure bear skirt at waist.

MAMA BEAR'S APRON

1. Layer the lining and apron pieces, wrong sides together. These will be dealt with as a single piece. Apply bias tape (page 13) to finish the rounded edge of Mama Bear's apron.

2. Cut 2 pieces 3½″ × 5½″ for apron pocket and pocket lining. Pin the pocket and lining right sides together and stitch around top and side edges. Trim corners and turn right side out. Fold the open bottom edges of the pocket and lining ¼″ to the inside and press. Pin in place and topstitch around the sides and bottom of the pocket.

3. Cut a piece 2½″ × 5⅛″ for apron waistband. Align the waistband at the top edge of the apron, with the right side of the waistband facing the back side of the apron. Pin and then sew.

4. Press a small hem on the short ends of the waistband. Press a small hem on the bottom edge of the waistband and then fold the waistband over to the front side of the apron. Edgestitch the waistband in place to the apron front.

5. Sew the apron securely to Mama Bear's torso at the top and side edges of the apron using a ladder stitch.

PAPA BEAR'S PANTS

1. Pin 2 pant legs together and sew the front seam, creating a pants panel. Repeat for the remaining leg pieces, creating a second panel.

2. Place the 2 pants panels together, aligning the front seams. Pin all the way around.

3. Sew from one edge of the pants, all the way down the leg, across the bottom of a pant leg, up the inside leg, and then all the way around the opposite leg in the same manner.

4. Clip seam allowances and turn right side out. Fold the raw edges of the waist ¼″ toward the inside and close with a ladder stitch.

5. Secure the pants to Papa Bear's waist with a ladder stitch.

PAPA BEAR'S VEST

1. Pin vest pieces to Papa Bear's torso and secure them at the shoulder and at the torso sides, along the seam.

2. Secure the front of the vest with 2 buttons.

GOLDILOCKS' APRON

1. Pin 2 apron pieces together, adding trim along the curved edge, if desired, and sew.

2. Clip the seam allowances and turn the apron right side out.

3. Cut a piece 1¾″ × 34″ for apron sash. Fold the apron sash in half lengthwise, wrong sides facing, and press. Unfold and press ¼″ hems along the length of both sides of the sash, and then fold the apron sash together once more.

4. Pin the sash to the apron, making sure to match the centers of the sash and the apron.

5. Turn in the raw edges of the apron sash ends and edgestitch the sash, making sure that the sash is securely attached to the apron.

6. Tie the apron to Goldilocks' waist.

Finish the Doll

1. Embroider Mama and Papa Bear's features using wool felt eyes approximately ⅜˝ in diameter and coordinating embroidery floss. Use a triangular piece of wool felt for each nose and whipstitch in place or embroider using a satin stitch.

2. Sew Baby Bear wool felt pieces wrong sides together using a whipstitch. Leave a small opening, stuff lightly with wool, and whipstitch the opening closed. Use a satin stitch to embroider simple features on Baby Bear following the template pattern.

Variations

Many different versions of a topsy-turvy doll can be made. In a manner similar to this project, try Little Red Riding Hood (pages 77–81) with Grandma and the wolf on one end and Little Red on the other. Or attach two torsos (or make one long torso with heads at both ends) and make a Snow White and Rose Red or Alice and the Red Queen.

how kids can help

I distinctly remember the Baby Bear that was part of the topsy-turvy Goldilocks doll my mother made so many years ago. I deliberately created an equally simple Baby Bear, one that a child could easily make alone or with little assistance. For those children new to sewing, make holes using a ¹⁄₁₆˝ craft punch. For kids with basic hand-sewing skills, let them whipstitch the bear independently.

Sew Baby Bear.

Bedtime Storytelling Cone Puppet

Finished size: 28˝ tall (the dowel can be made shorter, if desired)

Perfect for bedside entertainment, this playful puppet provides a fun way to narrate nighttime stories. I love watching my youngest daughter's eyes as she intently follows the puppet's movements until she quietly drifts off into peaceful slumber. Well, maybe not that last part. Who is dreaming now … ?

Instructions

Make the Head

1. Follow the instructions for *Sadie, Mae, and Elsie* (pages 59 and 60) for sewing the puppet head. Keep in mind that there is no torso or "bottom" piece.

2. Refer to Stuffing and Finishing (page 13) for general tips about stuffing. Stuff the head and neck firmly and use your fingers, a stuffing tool, or a felting needle to create a space for the wooden dowel.

3. Place a few drops of craft glue inside the head.

notes:

- Use the template patterns on page 152, and pullout page P3.

- Read all the project instructions before beginning the project.

- Refer to Tools and Techniques (pages 9–13) as needed.

- Trace all pattern pieces onto freezer paper (page 11).

- Press freezer-paper templates to the fabric and cut out the fabric pieces before removing the freezer-paper templates.

- Pieces are sewn together with right sides facing, unless otherwise noted.

- Use a short stitch length.

- The seam allowances are ³⁄₁₆˝, unless otherwise noted.

4. Insert the dowel and use a few drops of craft glue and some strong craft thread to secure the material around the dowel several times. Figure A.

5. Refer to All About Faces and Hair (pages 17–42) and embroider the facial features using black and red embroidery floss. Sew on the ears and add your preferred yarn hairstyle.

Make the Nightgown

1. Iron interfacing to back side of the nightgown fabric (*optional*) and cut out the nightgown front and back pieces.

2. Align and pin the straight edge of a hand to the end of a sleeve of the nightgown and sew. Repeat for the other 3 sleeve edges. Figure B.

3. Place the 2 nightgown pieces together, pin and sew from the bottom of the nightgown to the neck edge. Repeat for the other side. Figure C.

4. Finish the seams, clipping and notching where necessary, and turn right side out.

5. Finger-press the neck edge toward the inside of the nightgown.

Make the Nightcap

1. Place a sock on the puppet's head. Fit it to the head, like a hat, placing the elastic top of the sock around the head and the heel toward the back of the head.

2. Mark the sock with a pin showing where the top of the head is located. Remove the sock from the head.

3. Turn the sock inside out, and sew a line from the pin to the toe of the sock. Turn right side out.

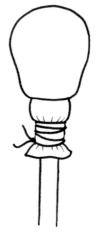

Figure A. Secure cone puppet head.

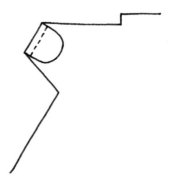

Figure B. Sew hands to nightgown.

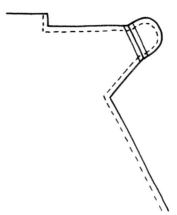

Figure C. Sew nightgown sides.

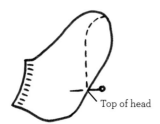

Top of head

Sew nightcap from sock.

4. Use coordinating thread and a doll needle to sew the nightcap securely to the puppet's head. Take a series of stitches around the lower edge of the nightcap (going through the whole doll head at times) to secure in place.

5. Tie a little string or thin ribbon around the end of the sock hat (*optional*).

Make the Cone Base

Note: Use Timtex for both the A and B pieces of the cone base. Piece B is slightly smaller so it can fit inside of piece A, providing added rigidity to the cone base.

1. With the straight edges aligned, sew piece A together using a ⅛˝ seam allowance. Repeat for piece B.

2. Gently press the seam of piece A to give the base a more rounded shape. Repeat for piece B.

3. Trim a small opening, large enough for the dowel, at the points of both cone bases.

4. Place piece B (with the seam allowances to the outside) inside of piece A. Adjust the 2 pieces so the seams are on opposite sides of the cone. This helps give the cone a better shape.

5. Use your hands to gently shape the cone base.

Make the Cone Cover

1. Align and pin the straight edges of the wool felt cone cover. Sew using a ⅛˝ seam allowance.

2. Turn the cone cover right side out (with the seam to the inside of the cone).

3. Pin the stars and moon around the cone covering. See the photo (page 92) for general placement. (I used 6 small stars and 4 large stars.)

4. Sew the stars and moon using a whipstitch (page 14) or any other preferred embroidery technique.

5. Embroider a face and craters on the moon if desired.

Assemble the Cone Puppet

1. Pin the bottom edge of the nightgown around the outer top edge of the cone base (piece A).

2. With a needle and strong thread, hand baste the nightgown edge to the cone. Use the neck opening for access to the inside of the cone base when hand sewing.

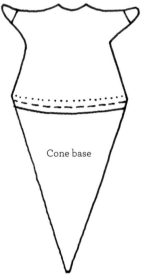

Cone base

Baste nightgown to cone base.

3. Place the cone base inside the felt cone cover. Place the seams of the cone base at the sides and the seam of the cover at the back.

4. Gently shape the cone again to achieve a more rounded look.

5. Blanket stitch (page 15) around the top edge of the cone, catching the cover, the nightgown, and the cone base (piece A).

6. Place the dowel and head inside of the nightgown's neck edge, with the dowel exiting the bottom of the cone.

7. Sew the neck edge of the nightgown to the cone puppet neck using a ladder stitch (page 14). Hand gather the nightgown neck as you sew to make it fit.

8. Whipstitch together the 2 smallest wool felt stars. As you sew, glue a toothpick or mini wooden dowel into the middle of the star to make a wand.

9. Fold a hand of the puppet in half to hold the wand. Stitch the hand and the wand in place.

how kids can help

This project offers a great opportunity to demonstrate to your child how to blanket stitch. You may want to let a younger child help pull the needle and floss after each stitch has been taken; an older child may be able to take the stitches independently.

Variations

Like so many of the other doll projects in this book, this cone puppet design can be easily modified to become a variety of different characters. Try a clown that pops out of a cone covered with brightly colored dots. A fairy godmother? A princess? A wizard? A fortune teller? Use your imagination and have fun dreaming up your own creation.

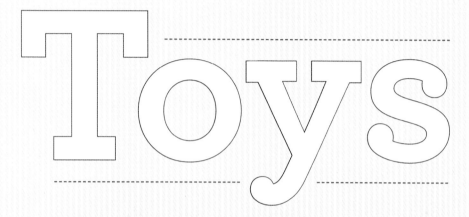

Toys

The following eight projects were inspired by stuffed toys, sewing patterns, and illustrations from the 1940s and 50s. From a sweet kitten pillow to a hand-sewn elephant sewing caddy, this section offers an assortment of delightful projects suitable for beginners as well as those more experienced with sewing.

Kitten Pillows

Finished sizes: Small kitten pillow is 10˝ in diameter; large kitten pillow is 14˝

N ot only popular during the 1940s and 50s, pillows of this type have reappeared throughout the decades and continue to be seen today. Moreover, they are appealing to both younger and older kids and are enticing propped up on a bed or nestled in a reading nook.

⅓ yard fabric for small pillow *or* ½ yard for large pillow (Cotton-linen, corduroy, or other durable fabric is recommended.)

⅔ yard light- to midweight fusible interfacing for small pillow *or* 1 yard for large pillow (especially if quilting-weight cotton fabric is used)

Black wool felt scraps for eyes

Pink wool felt scrap for nose

#5 black perle cotton or embroidery floss for features

White embroidery floss for eye highlight

10″ *or* 14″ round pillow form

Instructions

Make the Pillow

1. Turn under ½″ and then turn under ½″ again on the flat edge of both back pillow pieces. Press and topstitch hems. Hand baste the 2 back pieces together at the top and bottom to form a circle—use the front pillow pattern piece as a guide. Set the back piece aside.

2. Cut the eyes from wool felt and stitch a highlight in each eye by taking a few stitches with white floss.

3. Temporarily glue or hand baste the eyes in place using the template pattern as a guide.

notes:

- *Use the template patterns on pullout page P1.*

- *Read all the project instructions before beginning the project.*

- *Refer to Tools and Techniques (pages 9–13) as needed.*

- *Trace all pattern pieces onto freezer paper (page 11).*

- *Press freezer-paper templates to the fabric and cut out the fabric pieces before removing the freezer-paper templates.*

- *Pieces are sewn together with right sides facing, unless otherwise noted.*

- *The seam allowances are ¼″, unless otherwise noted.*

- *Fuse the interfacing to the back of the fabric before cutting out the pillow pieces.*

4. Pin the eyes to the pillow front (see template pattern for placement) and topstitch using matching thread.

5. Repeat Steps 3 and 4 for the nose.

6. Embroider the eyebrows and mouth with black perle cotton or embroidery floss. Add three whiskers on each side of the face.

7. Pin 2 ear pieces together and sew, leaving the bottom edge open. Clip the corner, turn right side out, and press. Repeat for the other ear.

8. Pin the ears in place with raw edges matching (see template pattern for placement) and then pin the front to the back and sew all the way around the pillow.

9. Notch the curves and trim seam allowances as needed.

10. Turn the pillow cover through the envelope back closure.

11. Insert the pillow form. If your pillow form has a zipper, you can open it and add extra stuffing if needed.

Variations

Such a simple design can be transformed into so many variations. How about a dog, a pig, or a little girl's (or boy's) face? Or try a sleeping kitty, perfect to snuggle up to in the evening.

how kids can help

This is truly a beginner project—one that a child who is comfortable with a sewing machine should be able to handle with minimal guidance and assistance from you (make sure you iron the back double hems). The features are the only tricky part for a child, but these can be sewn by hand if your child would like to complete the project independently (or the features can be simplified). Two circle pieces can also be sewn together, rather than making an envelope back, to make an even simpler design for kids. Leave an opening in the pillow's seam. Turn the pillow cover through the opening, insert the pillow form or use stuffing, and hand sew the opening closed.

Little Girl Purse

Finished size: Face is 6½˝; purse is 11˝ high (including the straps)

Inspiration for this project initially came from what I thought was a purse but was actually the *pocket* on a vintage girl's dress from the 1940s. After encouraging approval from my youngest daughter, who loved the test version, I went ahead and included this project in the collection of patterns. It is a fun way to test embroidery skills and customize a sweet little handbag for a young girl in your life.

materials

1 piece 8˝ × 8˝ cotton fabric for face	2 pieces 8˝ × 12˝ wool felt for hair and handles	1 piece 8˝ × 8˝ lightweight fusible interfacing
2 pieces 8˝ × 8˝ cotton fabric for purse lining	2 pieces 8˝ × 8˝ cotton batting	Embroidery floss for face
		Embroidery hoop

Instructions

Embroider the Face

1. Following the manufacturer's directions, iron lightweight interfacing to the back of the 8˝ × 8˝ piece of face fabric.

2. Place the face fabric on top of the face pattern and transfer all pattern marks, including the shape of the face and the facial features, to the right side. *Do not cut out the face shape yet.*

3. Place the piece of fabric in an embroidery hoop and embroider the facial features. Refer to All About Faces and Hair (pages 16–24) as needed.

4. Cut out the shape of the face, following the pattern.

5. Mist lightly with water to remove any air-erasable or water-soluble marks.

6. Press the face piece, if needed, only *after* the

notes:

- *Use the template patterns on page 153.*

- *Read all the project instructions before beginning the project.*

- *Refer to Tools and Techniques (pages 9–13) as needed.*

- *Trace all pattern pieces onto freezer paper (page 11).*

- *Press freezer-paper templates to the fabric, including the batting, and cut out the fabric pieces (except for the face fabric) before removing the freezer-paper templates. See instructions (at left) for the face pattern.*

- *Pieces are sewn together with right sides facing, unless otherwise noted.*

- *The seam allowances are ¼˝, unless otherwise noted.*

fabric is dry and all the air-erasable or water-soluble marks have disappeared.

Prepare the Outer Purse

1. Pin the wool felt front hair piece on top of the face and edge-stitch, following the bottom edge of the hairstyle.

2. Sew the 2 ponytail pieces, wrong sides together, using a ⅛˝ seam allowance, with stitching line showing on the outside.

3. Place the face and back of hair together, right sides facing.

4. Insert ponytails according to the pattern marks, or angle them to your preference.

5. Sew around the face, according to pattern marks, leaving the top of the purse open. Trim the seam allowances. *Do not turn right side out yet.*

Make the Purse Lining and Handles

1. Place the 2 purse lining pieces together, right sides facing, between 2 pieces of cotton batting, and pin all 4 layers (or hand baste). Sew around the edges of the purse lining, leaving the opening at the top and the *opening at the bottom* (for turning) as designated on the template pattern. Trim the seam allowances. Turn right side out.

2. Cut 2 pieces of felt 1½˝ × 11½˝ for the purse handles. Fold a handle in half lengthwise, wrong sides together, and sew with a ⅛˝ seam allowance. Repeat for the other handle.

3. Place the lining, right side out, inside the purse, which is still inside out. Insert purse handles in place as indicated on the pattern. Place the handles upside down (in a U shape) between the purse lining and the outer purse covering. Extend the purse's handles ¼˝ beyond the raw edges of the purse and lining.

4. Pin around the top edges and sew the purse and the lining together. Sew twice to reinforce the handles.

Handles

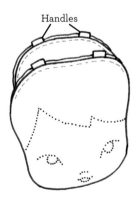

Finish the Purse

1. Trim the seam allowances around the upper edge of the purse.

2. Turn the purse right side out through the opening in the purse lining.

3. Hand sew the opening in the purse lining closed using a ladder stitch (page 14) and fit the lining inside the purse.

---

how kids can help

While there are a few projects in this book that would appeal to adults and kids alike, this is a project that is truly meant for kids. Involve your children with the design. Change the expression or hairstyle to their liking. Pick a fun material to line the purse with. They will likely be more proud to carry around a little bag that they helped to create.

Variations

Embroider the child's name on the back of the head. Change the look of the ponytails by trying out a whole new hairstyle, such as braids or small loops. Instead of a girl, make a purse that looks like your child's favorite animal. Or make a kitten purse, drawing on the techniques found in both this project and *Kitten Pillows* (pages 98–100).

Humpty

Finished size: 8″ tall including the hat

This nostalgic toy was inspired by vintage Humpty Dumpty toy patterns and nursery décor from the last century. Weighted with sand and fitted with legs that can bend, Humpty can easily perch on a shelf and adds a whimsical accent to any nursery or bedroom (or sewing space!). His felt trousers are even removable to reveal a cracked shell on his bottom end. This is a quick project, suitable for those newer to toymaking.

materials

1 piece 8˝ × 15˝ white cotton fabric for body

1 piece 8˝ × 15˝ fusible interfacing (suggested)

4˝ × 4˝ scrap of cotton woven fabric or wool felt for legs

Wool felt scraps for trousers, arms, hands, feet, and hat

1 piece 1¼˝ × 11³/₁₆˝ wool felt for collar

Stuffing

Sand for weighting

Black and red embroidery floss for features

1 pipe cleaner or chenille stem for legs

3 doll-sized buttons

Instructions

Make the Egg Body

1. Sew 2 pieces of the egg body together along a side. Repeat with the remaining 2 pieces, resulting in 2 halves.

2. Place the egg halves together and sew around the egg, leaving an opening for turning and stuffing, as designated on pattern. Refer to Stuffing and Finishing (page 13) for general tips about stuffing.

notes:

- *Use the template patterns on pages 152 and 153.*

- *Read all the project instructions before beginning the project.*

- *Refer to Tools and Techniques (pages 9–13) as needed.*

- *Iron fusible interfacing (suggested) to the white cotton fabric prior to cutting the egg body shapes.*

- *Trace all pattern pieces onto freezer paper (page 11).*

- *Press freezer-paper templates to the fabric and cut out the fabric pieces before removing the freezer-paper templates.*

- *Pieces are sewn together with right sides facing, unless otherwise noted.*

- *Use a short stitch length.*

- *The seam allowances are ³/₁₆˝, unless otherwise noted.*

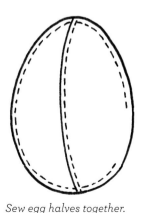

Sew egg halves together.

tip The facial features can be transferred prior to sewing the egg halves together. Likewise, they can be embroidered prior to any sewing, or after sewing is complete (but prior to stuffing). As mentioned on page 17, I prefer to work on the face after a toy is stuffed, so that is what is detailed here.

3. Trim the seam allowances and clip the curves.

4. Turn right side out, weight the bottom with a small woven bag of sand (*optional*; see Tip, page 13), and stuff.

5. Close the opening with a ladder stitch (page 14).

6. Transfer and embroider the facial features (pages 16–24). Hide the knots where the hat will be sewn on, or use the Tip (page 24) on "knotless" starts.

7. Embroider some jagged lines on Humpty's bottom to indicate a broken shell.

Make the Trousers and Arms

1. Sew together 2 trouser pieces with a ⅛˝ seam allowance along one rounded side. Sew the remaining 2 pieces together, resulting in 2 halves.

2. Place the halves together and sew along the curved edge.

3. Turn the trousers right side out, and pin the collar on the inside of the trousers, starting with an end of the collar centered at the top edge of the front trousers piece. Continue to pin around the entire inner edge of the trousers. Trim excess felt off the collar, if needed, so that the edges of the felt collar meet squarely in the center.

4. Edgestitch (by hand or machine) the collar in place at the upper edge of the trousers. You may find it easier to hand baste, then flip the trousers inside out and edgestitch on the machine.

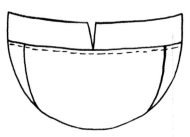

Stitch collar in place.

5. Fold an arm piece lengthwise, wrong sides together, and whipstitch (page 14). Repeat for the remaining arm.

6. Whipstitch 2 hands, wrong sides together, and whipstitch to the bottom of an arm. Repeat for the other hand and arm.

7. Securely hand sew the arms to the trousers, slightly below the collar on each side (see photo, page 104, for placement).

8. Fold the collar over the top pants edge. Sew 3 buttons to the center pants panel piece.

Make the Legs and Shoes

1. If you are using wool felt for legs, roll the felt (right side out) along the long edges to make a tube and whipstitch each leg individually.

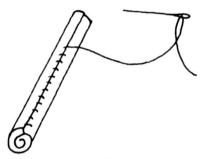

Whipstitch wool felt legs.

Or …

If you are using fabric, fold the fabric lengthwise, right sides together, and sew with a ⅛˝ seam allowance. Turn the legs right side out and fold the raw edges at the top of each leg inward.

2. Secure the tops of the legs to the trousers using a whipstitch.

3. Cut a pipe cleaner or chenille stem into 2 pieces 3˝ long and use tweezers to bend in both ends so they are not sharp or pointed.

4. Insert a pipe cleaner or chenille stem piece into each leg so that the legs can be bent.

5. Hand sew the straight edges of the upper shoe together to form the back of the shoe. Then whipstitch the upper shoe to the sole. Stuff lightly and repeat for remaining shoe.

6. Place the bottom of each leg into a shoe and whipstitch in place.

Make the Hat

1. Use pinking shears to cut the rounded edge of the hat (*optional*).

2. Join the 2 straight edges together and sew with a ⅛˝ seam allowance.

3. Turn right side out and fold up the edge of the hat by ½˝.

4. Hand sew the hat securely to the top of Humpty's head.

how kids can help

Embroidering the jagged lines on Humpty is a perfect step to involve your child, especially because the lines are supposed to be crooked! Kids can also help with stuffing the egg body and whipstitching the arms (and legs, if using wool felt).

Variations

Whip up an assortment of trousers and simple hats so your child can change Humpty's look from time to time. Include a little Santa or elf hat for the winter or bunny ears for the spring. An egg with bunny ears? Why not!

Roly-Poly Duck

Finished size: 8˝ tall

T though most often made of plastic, roly-poly tumble toys were commonly found in mid-century toy boxes. Ducks with little sailor hats were also quite popular, not just as toys but on greeting cards, storybooks, and other childhood treasures. Inspired by both trends, I created this wool felt version of a roly-poly toy. He is a fun addition to any playroom and relatively simple to make.

Instructions

Make the Duck Body

1. Pin and sew 2 duck body pieces together using a ⅛″ seam allowance along one side. Pin and sew a third piece, creating half of the body.

2. Repeat Step 1 for the remaining 3 pieces, resulting in the second half of the body.

3. Pin the halves together and sew all the way around, leaving a 2″ opening for stuffing. Refer to Stuffing and Finishing (page 13) for general tips about stuffing.

4. Turn right side out and add a small, securely sewn pouch of sand to weight, if desired. Add a rattle or noisemaker (*optional*).

5. Stuff firmly and close the opening with a ladder stitch (page 14).

notes:

- *Use the template patterns on pages 154 and 155.*

- *Read all the project instructions before beginning the project.*

- *Refer to Tools and Techniques (pages 9–13) as needed.*

- *Trace all pattern pieces onto freezer paper (page 11).*

- *Press freezer-paper templates to the fabric and cut out the fabric pieces before removing the freezer-paper templates.*

- *Pieces are sewn together with right sides facing, unless otherwise noted.*

- *Use a short stitch length.*

- *The seam allowances are ⅛″, unless otherwise noted.*

Make the Duck Head

1. Pin a side of the duck head to the center gusset, matching the marks on the pattern, and sew using a ⅛″ seam allowance. Repeat for other side.

2. Turn right side out and stuff firmly.

3. Make a knot at the end of an arm's-length piece of upholstery thread and hand sew a running stitch (page 14) approximately ⅛″ from the bottom edge all the way around the duck's head. Pull the thread to gather it tightly around the bottom, pushing the stuffing inside with a stuffing fork or the end of a pencil or wooden spoon.

4. Add more stuffing if necessary to make a firm, round head.

5. Repeat the running stitches slightly above the original stitches if needed for a more secure gather.

6. Sew the duck head to the duck body using a ladder stitch.

Make the Duck Hat

1. Place 2 hat pieces together and sew along a longer side. Add a third piece in the same manner to make half of the hat. Repeat using the remaining 3 pieces to make the other half of the hat.

2. Place the 2 halves together and sew, creating a dome-shaped hat.

3. Sew the 2 brim pieces together along the outer curved edge.

4. Align the 2 straight edges of the brim, right sides facing, and sew. Turn the brim right side out. Press.

5. Sew the inner curved (raw) edge of the brim to the edge of the hat.

6. Fold the seam allowance to the inside and topstitch with the seam allowance toward the hat.

7. Fold up the brim to make a sailor hat.

Make the Collar

1. Pin the 2 collar pieces together and sew around the edges, leaving an area open for turning.

2. Notch the curves and trim the corners.

3. Turn and press.

4. Close the opening with a ladder stitch.

Make the Duck Bill

1. Place the inner upper duck bill inside the outer duck bill, aligning the top curved edges.

2. Fold the outer duck bill in half and, using coordinating thread, take 3 stitches on the side edge using a blanket stitch (page 15), sewing all 3 layers of felt together. This will hold the edge of the bill together.

3. After 3 stitches, use the blanket stitch and continue to sew around the front top edge of the bill, sewing only the inner upper bill to the outer upper bill. This creates the upper duck bill.

4. As you near the other side, fold up the lower bill and use the blanket stitch to sew all 3 layers together once again.

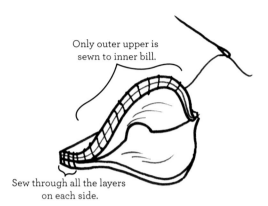

Only outer upper is sewn to inner bill.

Sew through all the layers on each side.

5. Sew the folded upper edge of the duck bill to the head. Place a pin inside the bill to help hold it in place and whipstitch (page 14), shaping the bill with your fingers (pushing the sides toward each other to form an upper curve).

6. Sew the inside of the bill to the head at the center semicircle with a few stitches, making what looks like the inside of the duck's mouth. Continue to sew around the entire bill to ensure it is secured to the head.

Make the Hands

1. Use upholstery thread to hand sew a small running stitch (page 14) around the edge of the circle, about ⅛˝ from the circle's edge.

2. Gather and stuff, continuing to stuff as the stitches are pulled tighter.

3. Make another row of running stitches (near the original stitches) for added strength.

4. Sew the hand securely to the duck body using a ladder stitch.

5. Repeat for the other hand.

Finish the Toy

1. Embroider black circles or ovals for eyes (see photo, page 108, for placement) using a satin stitch (page 15).

2. Secure the hat to the top of the head.

3. Tie the sailor collar around the neck.

how kids can help

"How did you do that?" Sometimes my girls just enjoy watching a certain technique. Observing how a running stitch can turn wool felt circles into three-dimensional shapes can actually provide its own teachable moment. Ask them to pull the thread as the duck hand comes together or have them stuff while you pull the thread. It's an easy step, but involving your little ones provides them with extra skills that they can then use with their own scrap baskets and thread.

Variations

The general shape of this toy can be easily modified to create a whole cast of roly-poly characters. Make a circus clown and add a ruffle around its neck. Perhaps create a roly-poly Santa or a snowman for wintertime.

Cottontail

Finished size: Approximately 9˝ long

I have a particular fondness for rabbits and was certain that a bunny was essential to this collection. I wanted to ensure that this bunny was not only reminiscent of a velveteen rabbit but also soft and cuddly—sure to become a preferred bedtime companion. The design was a hit with my girls and I hope this bunny will be cherished by your little ones as well.

¼ yard brown Minky or cotton velour fabric

¼ yard cream Minky or cotton velour fabric (I used organic sherpa, a soft, fluffy cotton fabric.)

Stuffing

Embroidery floss (I used pink, black, and white.)

Black wool felt scraps for eyes

½ yard lightweight fusible interfacing (*optional*, if using cotton velour)

Approximately ⅔ yard ¾˝-wide ribbon for bow (*optional*)

Instructions

Make the Ears

1. Pin a cream ear piece to a brown ear piece and sew, leaving the top straight edge open. Repeat for the other ear.

2. Clip the corners, trim the edges if needed, and turn both ears right side out.

3. Fold an ear in half lengthwise with inner ear inside, aligning the edges. Baste the raw edges of the folded ear. Cut the upper dart on the head down the middle, but do not sew it yet. Pin folded ear inside the upper dart of a side head piece. Make sure there is *at least ¼˝ of fabric* above the ear to allow for the seams of the head gusset.

notes:

- *Use the template patterns on pages 156 and 157.*

- *Read all the project instructions before beginning the project.*

- *Refer to Tools and Techniques (pages 9–13) as needed.*

- *Refer to Sewing with Knits (page 13).*

- *Trace all pattern pieces onto freezer paper (page 11).*

- *Iron interfacing onto the cotton velour fabric prior to cutting out pattern pieces to prevent curling of the raw edges.*

- *Press pattern pieces to the fabric, and cut out the fabric pieces before removing the freezer-paper templates.*

- *Pieces are sewn together with right sides facing, unless otherwise noted.*

- *The seam allowances are ¼˝, unless otherwise noted.*

4. Sew the dart and ear in place. Repeat for the remaining ear and side head piece.

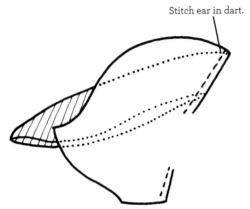

Stitch ear in dart.

Sew ears to side head darts.

5. Sew both lower side head darts.

Make the Head

1. Pin the side head pieces right sides together and sew from the nose down to the neck.

2. Sew the dart on the head gusset.

3. Pin the head gusset in place between the side pieces. Hand baste around the curve of the nose if necessary. (Hand basting the whole head gusset in place takes a few minutes more but makes this step *much easier.*) Sew, taking care not to catch the ears in the seam.

Head gusset

4. Finish the seams, clipping the curves and notches. Turn the head right side out.

Make the Body

1. Sew the inner and outer tail pieces together. Clip the seam allowances and turn right side out. Fold the tail in half, with the cream fabric on the inside and raw edges aligned, and baste.

2. Pin together the back seam of the outer body pieces. Position the tail in place near the bottom (along the straight edge) of the back seam. Make sure to allow for a seam allowance of at least ¼″ at the bottom of the outer body pieces.

3. Sew the back seam of the outer body pieces, making sure to leave an opening in the back as designated on the pattern piece.

4. Pin and then sew the inner body pieces together along the center belly seam.

5. Pin the inner body to the outer body from a neck edge all the way around the arms and the legs to the other side of the neck.

6. Sew all the way around, leaving the neck open.

7. Finish the seams as needed, making sure to clip the corners near the arms and feet. *Do not turn right side out.*

Attach the Head

1. Place the head, upside down and right side out, inside the bunny body, so that the right sides are facing. Align the front center head seam with the center belly seam at the raw edges. Align the head gusset dart with the center back seam and pin in place. Pin or hand baste (strongly recommended) the rest of the neck edges in place.

2. Sew the head and body together around the neck edge, and then turn right side out through the opening in the back seam.

Stuff and Embroider the Features

1. Refer to Stuffing and Finishing (page 13) for general tips about stuffing. Stuff the bunny.

2. Close the back opening with a ladder stitch (page 14).

3. Cut 2 black circles of felt approximately ⅜″ in diameter. Whipstitch (page 14) the eyes in place with black floss, and add a white dot to each eye. Embroider a simple pink nose. You may embroider eyes instead of using felt.

how kids can help

Have your child help sew up the back of the bunny using a ladder stitch. The plush velour or Minky fabric allows any crooked stitches to blend in a bit better than would a crisp woven. Demonstrate the stitch and see if your little one wants to give it a try.

Variations

Use white or pastel fabrics for a springtime bunny! Weight with a small bag of sand or add a pouch of lavender for a relaxing scent that will help your little one drift off to sleep.

Spot

Finished size: 15˝ long

Spot is a practical and fun toy for either a boy or a girl, a bedside protector at night and a pajama (or secret treasure!) holder during the day. What child wouldn't want this sweet puppy to snuggle next to?

materials

1 yard corduroy fabric for body	⅓ yard or 2 pieces 10˝ × 12˝ cotton fabric for pocket lining	Wool felt scraps for features and coordinating embroidery floss

Stuffing

Instructions

Make the Head and Upper Body

1. Sew 2 ear pieces (A) together along the curved edge. Leave the straight edge open for turning. Clip and notch the curves and turn right side out. Repeat for the other ear.

2. Cut the upper dart where indicated on a side head piece (B). Pin an ear into the dart, making sure to allow for a ¼˝ seam allowance on the top, and sew the dart. Repeat for the remaining ear and side head piece.

3. Sew the lower neck darts on both side head pieces, using a ⅛˝ seam allowance.

4. Pin the 2 side head pieces together at the nose and down to the neck.

5. *Sew only the top 1¼˝ of the nose*, following the pattern marks.

notes:

- *Use the template patterns on pullout pages P3 and P4.*

- *Read all the project instructions before beginning the project.*

- *Refer to Tools and Techniques (pages 9–13) as needed.*

- *Trace all pattern pieces onto freezer paper (page 11).*

- *Press freezer-paper templates to wrong side of the fabric, and cut out the fabric pieces before removing the freezer-paper templates. For the side head piece, ears, and tail, press the freezer-paper templates to the wrong side of a folded length of fabric and cut 2 pieces at a time.*

- *Pieces are sewn together with right sides facing, unless otherwise noted.*

- *The seam allowances are ¼˝, unless otherwise noted.*

6. Remove the rest of the pins and place the lower head gusset (C) so the marked center of the curved edge aligns with the lower nose seam. Hand baste or pin the rest of the curve to the lower head gusset and lower face edges, and sew.

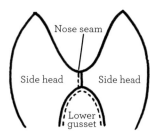

7. Sew the dart on the top head gusset (D), using a ⅛˝ seam allowance.

8. Pin the top head gusset in place between the 2 side head pieces. Hand baste around the curve of the upper nose, if necessary. Sew the center head gusset.

9. Clip and notch the curves, trim the seam allowances as needed, and turn the head right side out.

10. Sew the dart in the upper body (E), near the puppy's back end, using a ⅛˝ seam allowance.

11. Align and pin the lower edge of the head inside the neck opening of the upper body piece. Make sure that the head is centered, or positioned in a way that is appealing to you. Sew it in place around the circular neck opening.

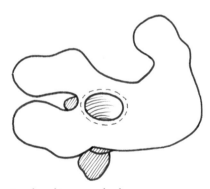

Sew head to upper body.

Make the Underbody and Pajama Pocket

1. Sew the underbody pieces (F1 and F2) together along the straight edge. At the opening (designated on the pattern), stop in the needle-down position at the marked lines and pivot the fabric 90°. Sew toward the raw edge, making a right angle with the previous seam.

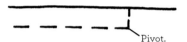

Sew toward raw edge.

2. Pin the pocket pieces (G) together and sew around the edges. Note the pattern markings and leave a 6˝ opening at the top for the pocket opening and a 4˝ opening at the bottom for turning right side out. Near the pocket openings, follow the steps above and pivot the fabric to sew at a right angle toward the raw edges.

tip The finished pocket is large enough to hold a small child's nightshirt or toddler-sized pajamas. If a larger pocket is desired, simply cut larger rectangles of fabric and transfer the measurements for the pocket openings at both the opening and bottom edges.

3. Clip near the angled seamlines at the pocket openings, and pin the pocket and the underbody together, right sides facing. Sew the pocket opening all the way around.

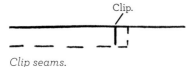

Clip seams.

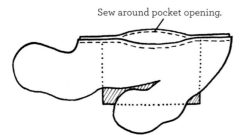

Sew underbody and pocket.

Make the Body

1. Pin the 2 tail pieces (H) together; sew, leaving the bottom edge open. Trim the seam allowances where needed and turn the tail right side out.

2. Align and pin the lower back leg gusset (I) to the lower back leg (F2), and sew between the pattern dots.

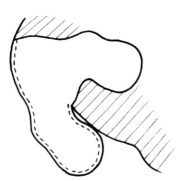

Sew inner lower leg to lower back leg.

3. Pin the side inner upper back leg to the outer upper back leg and continue to pin all the way around the body. Make sure to also position the tail in place, where marked on the upper body piece, approximately ¼˝ above the back dart.

4. Sew around the whole body.

5. Clip the notches, curves, and corners, and finish the seam allowances as needed.

6. Turn the body right side out through the opening at the bottom of the pocket.

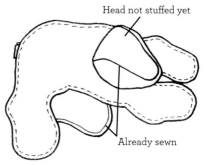

Sew all around.

Stuff

1. Refer to Stuffing and Finishing (page 13) for general tips about stuffing. Fill the head with wool or a soft polyfill stuffing through the bottom opening in the pocket lining.

2. Stuff the paws of the puppy, stuff just a bit of its legs, and lightly stuff its backside. Leave the puppy loosely stuffed and keep in mind that the rest of the puppy will usually be stuffed by a nightgown or pajamas.

3. Close the opening at the bottom of the pocket with a ladder stitch (page 14).

how kids can help

This is a project whose stuffing could be done almost entirely by a child. There are no contoured faces to pack, no bodies, arms, or legs that you are trying to make smooth. And stuffing is a task that kids (mine, at least) seem to enjoy. Have them lightly stuff the paws and even help with stuffing the head. The puppy should feel floppy and soft.

tip If the neck is left open inside the body, stuffing will occasionally shift around. This is easily fixed by placing your hand inside the pocket and pushing the stuffing back into place from time to time. But if the puppy is a gift or you just want to avoid having to do this, cut a circle slightly larger than the neck opening. Go in through the opening at the bottom of the pocket and pin the circle of fabric to the inner raw edges of the neck. (Make sure the head is stuffed first!) Whipstitch the edges in place.

Finish the Toy

1. Position the wool felt features and sew them into place using a whipstitch (page 14).

2. Slightly bend the ears to position them in place and tack them to the head, if desired.

Variations

Add a zipper closure or, with a simple change of the ears, turn this project into cat! Embroider your child's name on the upper back or other features on the puppy, such as whiskers or lines on its paws to suggest toes.

Henry

Finished size: 12″ tall

Henry is a charming horse inspired by a vintage birthday card that I pinned to my bulletin board years ago. Made of corduroy, wool felt, and yarn, this delightful toy is sure to appeal to kids and horse lovers of all ages.

Instructions

Make the Hooves and Ears

1. Pin a hoof to the right side of an outer horse leg and topstitch across the top of the hoof. Repeat for the remaining 3 legs.

2. Repeat Step 1 to sew the remaining hooves to the inner horse legs.

3. Pin 2 ear pieces together. If using contrasting fabric for the inner ear, pin an outer and an inner ear together. Sew, leaving the bottom edge open. Repeat for the other ear.

4. Clip the corners and notch the curves, if needed, and turn both ears right side out.

5. Fold an ear in half lengthwise with the inner

notes:

- Use the template patterns on pullout page P1.

- Read all the project instructions before beginning the project.

- Refer to Tools and Techniques (pages 9–13) as needed.

- Trace all pattern pieces onto freezer paper (page 11).

- Press freezer-paper templates to the fabric and cut out the fabric pieces before removing the freezer-paper templates.

- Pieces are sewn together with right sides facing, unless otherwise noted.

- Use a short stitch length and sew seams twice for durability.

- The seam allowances are ¼˝, unless otherwise noted.

ear inside, aligning the bottom raw edges. Baste the bottom edge of the folded ear. Cut the dart line at the top of the horse's head as indicated on the pattern. Pin the folded ear inside the dart. *The ear should be angled upward* and the basted ear seam should be within the seam allowance of the dart. Make sure there is also at least ¼˝ of fabric above the ear for a seam allowance.

6. Sew the dart and ear in place. Repeat for the remaining ear and side.

Make and Sew the Mane

1. Follow the directions for making a sewn wig in All About Faces and Hair (pages 37–39) and make a short looped wig for the mane. I used a piece of cardboard 2¾˝ × 7˝ (with a ⅝˝ piece cut out down the middle) and wrapped the yarn strands tightly next to each other for 4½˝.

2. Remove the sewn wig and trim ½˝ from the yarn on a side of the stitched line (*only half the loops will become the mane*).

3. Cut down the center of the dart of the head gusset. Align the stitched, trimmed part of the mane within the dart, making sure that the mane's stitched line is within the seam allowance of the dart.

4. Sew the dart twice. Trim any excess yarn from the underside of the head gusset, as needed. Trim the mane's loops *after* the horse has been stuffed.

Make the Underbody and Center Gusset

1. Sew the 4 leg darts on the underbody pieces. Reinforce the darts by sewing a second time (recommended).

2. Sew the underbody pieces together along the upper curved edge, leaving an opening in the center, as designated on the pattern piece. Leave the angled straight upper edges unsewn.

3. Pin the short straight upper edge of the underbody unit to the straight edge of the head gusset piece and sew.

Sew the Underbody and Head Gusset to the Sides

1. Pin and sew the underbody / head gusset unit to a side of the horse, from the pointed curve of the underbody gusset, located near the horse's backside, to the pointed edge of the head gusset, located at the back of the head. Take your time with this step. *I highly recommend carefully hand basting the nose area with a backstitch* (page 14). Basting makes sewing this area much easier and ensures a cleaner finish.

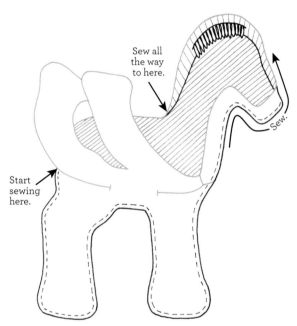

Sew all the way to here.

Start sewing here.

Sew.

Sew underbody / head gusset unit to horse side.

2. Pin the other side of the underbody/gusset unit to the opposite side of the horse and continue to pin all the way around the horse and sew, including the horse's back.

Pin and sew around horse.

3. Notch or clip the curves and trim seam allowances where needed.

4. Turn right side out through the opening in the underbody.

Finish the Toy

1. Stuff the horse firmly. Refer to Stuffing and Finishing (page 13) for general tips about stuffing.

2. Close the opening on the underbody with a ladder stitch (page 14).

3. Use a few tack stitches to secure a bundle or loops of yarn to the backside of the horse for the tail.

4. Trim the mane loops.

5. Sew on button eyes or embroider eyes if safety is a concern.

6. Place the 2 saddle pieces together, insert 3˝ of twill tape on each side of the saddle for ties, and sew, leaving a small opening for turning. Clip the seam allowances and turn right side out. Hand sew the opening closed and add a snap to the twill ties.

how kids can help

A simple saddle made from gingham fabric provides an easy cross-stitch lesson for your child. Those kids familiar with basic sewing techniques may be able to sew the saddle entirely on their own.

Variations

Add a simple horn and make a unicorn, or a set of wings to become Pegasus. Reduce or enlarge the pattern to create a stable full of horses.

Elephant Sewing Caddy

Finished size: 5˝ tall

Combing through an archive of vintage toy patterns, I stumbled upon a 1920s pattern of an elephant sewing caddy. It had a trunk that held a thimble and a blanket that held pins and needles. The style was quite different from the collection of toys sketched in my notebook, but the idea was compelling. So I designed this pattern with a more mid-century appeal and added accents such as a brightly colored pincushion and button-jointed legs that can be posed. This elephant would make a practical and playful gift for a child's sewing space, or even that of an adult who is young at heart.

Instructions

Make the Elephant Body

1. Fold the darts right sides together and sew the darts on the elephant side body and head gusset pieces using a small whipstitch.

2. With the darts facing the inside of the body, match A to B and sew the trunk gusset to a side of the body. Repeat for other side.

3. With the darts facing the inside of the body, align the dart of a center head gusset with the upper dart on the side head and whip-stitch from the back of the head toward the front end of the center head gusset. Repeat for the other side and continue to whipstitch all the way up to the end of the trunk.

notes:

- Use the template patterns on pages 158 and 159.

- Read all the project instructions before beginning the project.

- Refer to Tools and Techniques (pages 9–13) as needed.

- Trace all pattern pieces onto freezer paper (page 11).

- Press freezer-paper templates to the felt and cut out the felt pieces before removing the freezer-paper templates.

- This project is sewn by hand, using either a whipstitch (page 14) or a blanket stitch (page 15).

- All seams are stitched wrong sides together, leaving seam allowances on the outside, unless otherwise noted.

4. Sew the back together from the back point of the head gusset until you reach the back darts.

5. Match C to D and align the underbody gusset in place, positioning the underbody gusset on the *outside* of the trunk gusset. Sew each side. The underbody gusset will overlap the trunk and is wider at the mouth, so the mouth of the elephant will appear to be open. Start to stuff the elephant's head and then the body as you complete this step. Use the palm of your hand to cradle and shape the elephant's head as you stuff it firmly.

6. Finish stuffing and sewing the elephant body. Refer to Stuffing and Finishing (page 13) for general tips about stuffing.

7. Place the 2 short ends of the trunk lining together and whipstitch. Insert the trunk lining inside the trunk opening, test the fit with a thimble (placed inside the trunk opening), and adjust if necessary. Whipstitch around the upper edge of the trunk opening.

Make the Ears and Legs

1. Place 2 ear pieces together and sew around the outer edge. Repeat for the other 2 ear pieces. Place the ears on the head, covering the upper head dart, and sew them securely in place (refer to the photo on page 125).

2. Sew the legs by placing 2 leg pieces together and sewing from the bottom of a side around to the bottom of the other side.

3. Place the circular foot pad in place and start to sew to the bottom of the leg. Stuff the leg as you go until the foot pad is sewn on and the leg is sewn closed. Repeat for the remaining 3 legs.

4. Secure the legs to the elephant's sides using buttons and a doll needle to sew back and forth through the elephant's body, anchoring the front legs first and then the back legs.

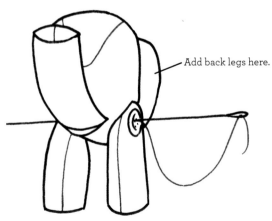

Add back legs here.

Attach legs.

Make the Elephant Details

1. Use pinking shears to trim the circular edge of the hat and then sew the straight edges of the hat together by hand or machine. Turn the seam to the inside and turn up the brim of the hat. Add some stuffing and secure the hat to the top of the elephant's head.

2. Pink the edges of the smaller blanket and sew it to the larger blanket with a running stitch (page 14) or other decorative stitch using embroidery floss. Add the rectangular piece to a side of the blanket to hold tiny scissors (if desired). Take a few stitches on each of the short sides of the blanket to secure in place to the elephant's body.

3. Fold the tail in half and whipstitch along the length. As you approach the curve, whipstitch the tail in place on the elephant's backside (refer to the photo below).

4. Sew the strawberry top to the strawberry (clipped off a tomato pincushion) and then whipstitch the bottom of the tail to the strawberry.

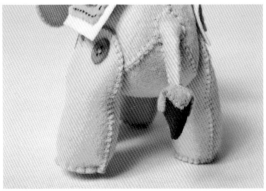

Sew on tail.

5. Embroider the elephant's eyes using small pieces of black wool felt and a few small stitches with black embroidery floss.

Make the Pincushion

1. Sew the triangles to the pincushion strip.

2. Sew the stars to the pincushion strip.

3. Sew the short ends of the strip together to form a ring.

4. Blanket stitch (page 15) the strip to the circular top and bottom bases; stuff while closing.

how kids can help

Just pulling the needle and thread can mean "helping" to many young ones. Take a stitch, hand the needle carefully over to your child, and have him or her help pull. For older children with some hand-sewing skills, have them assist with the pincushion or perhaps design one of their own!

Variations

This cheery elephant makes an adorable big-top addition to any nursery or playroom shelf. Instead of a sewing caddy, simply make the elephant a toy! Omit the blanket and fasten a sweet ruffled collar instead. (Be careful of the button-jointed legs with small children!)

template patterns

Little Cub
(project on page 44)

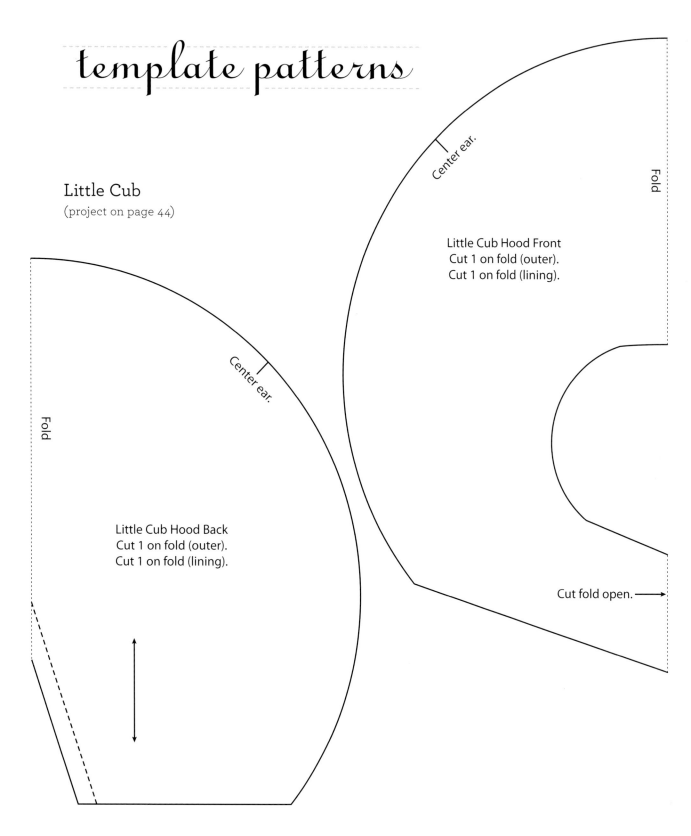

Center ear.

Little Cub Hood Front
Cut 1 on fold (outer).
Cut 1 on fold (lining).

Fold

Center ear.

Fold

Little Cub Hood Back
Cut 1 on fold (outer).
Cut 1 on fold (lining).

Cut fold open. →

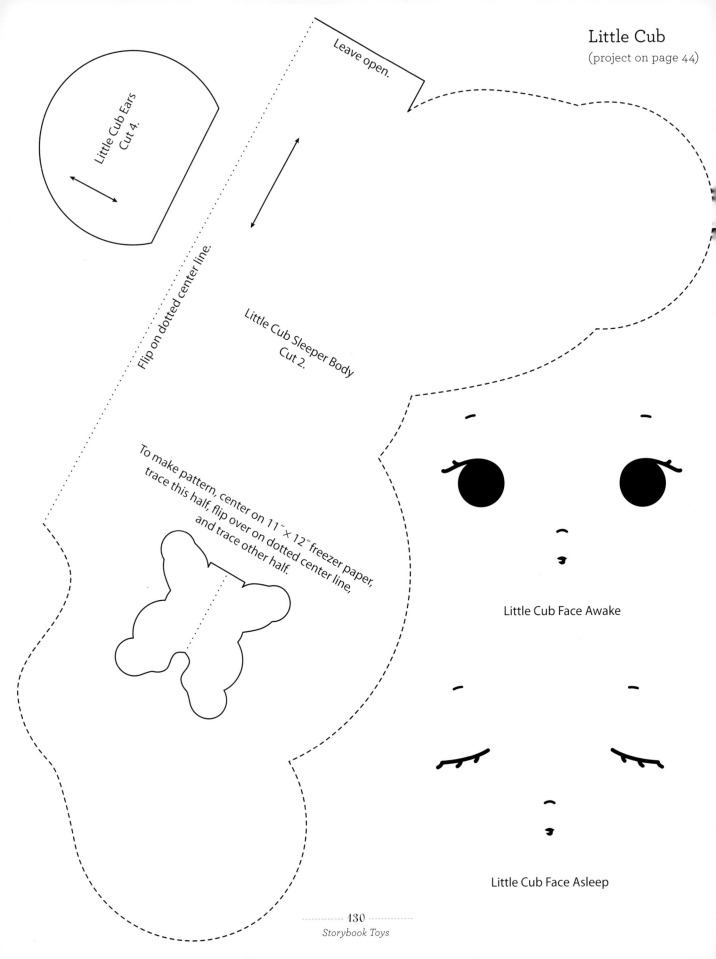

Little Cub
(project on page 44)

Little Cub Ears
Cut 4.

Leave open.

Flip on dotted center line.

Little Cub Sleeper Body
Cut 2.

To make pattern, center on 11″ × 12″ freezer paper, trace this half, flip over on dotted center line, and trace other half.

Little Cub Face Awake

Little Cub Face Asleep

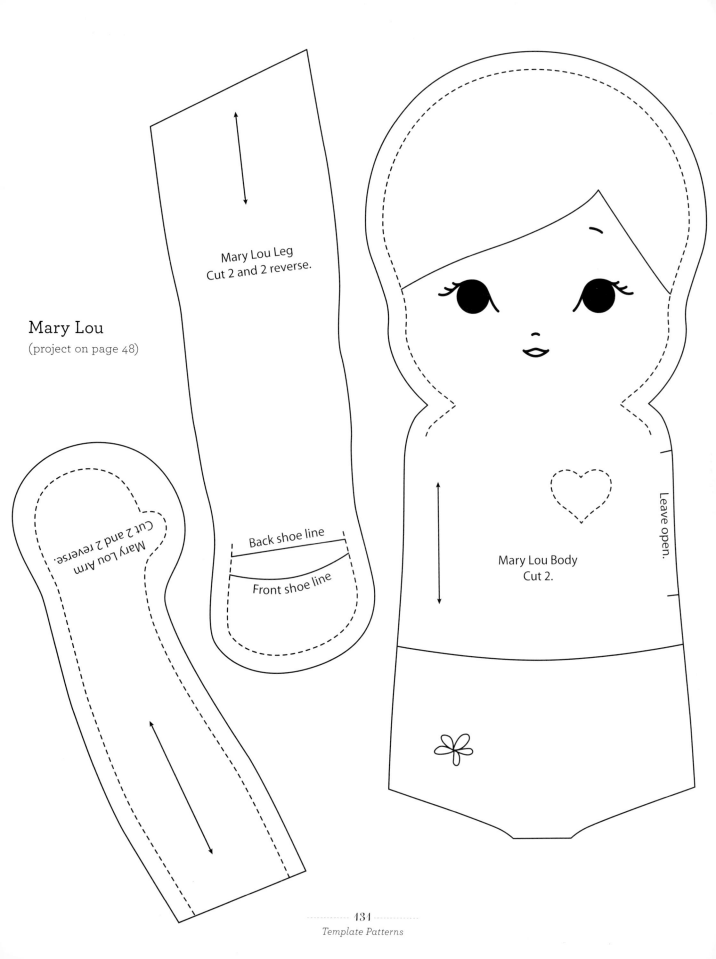

Mary Lou Leg
Cut 2 and 2 reverse.

Mary Lou

(project on page 48)

Mary Lou Arm
Cut 2 and 2 reverse.

Back shoe line

Front shoe line

Leave open.

Mary Lou Body
Cut 2.

Template Patterns

Mary Lou

(project on page 48)

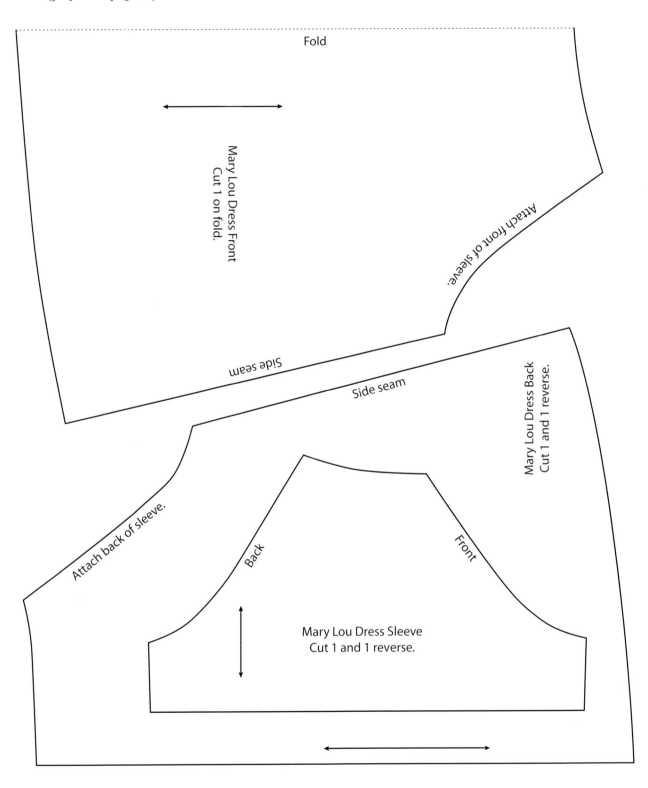

Fold

Mary Lou Dress Front
Cut 1 on fold.

Attach front of sleeve.

Side seam

Side seam

Mary Lou Dress Back
Cut 1 and 1 reverse.

Attach back of sleeve.

Back

Front

Mary Lou Dress Sleeve
Cut 1 and 1 reverse.

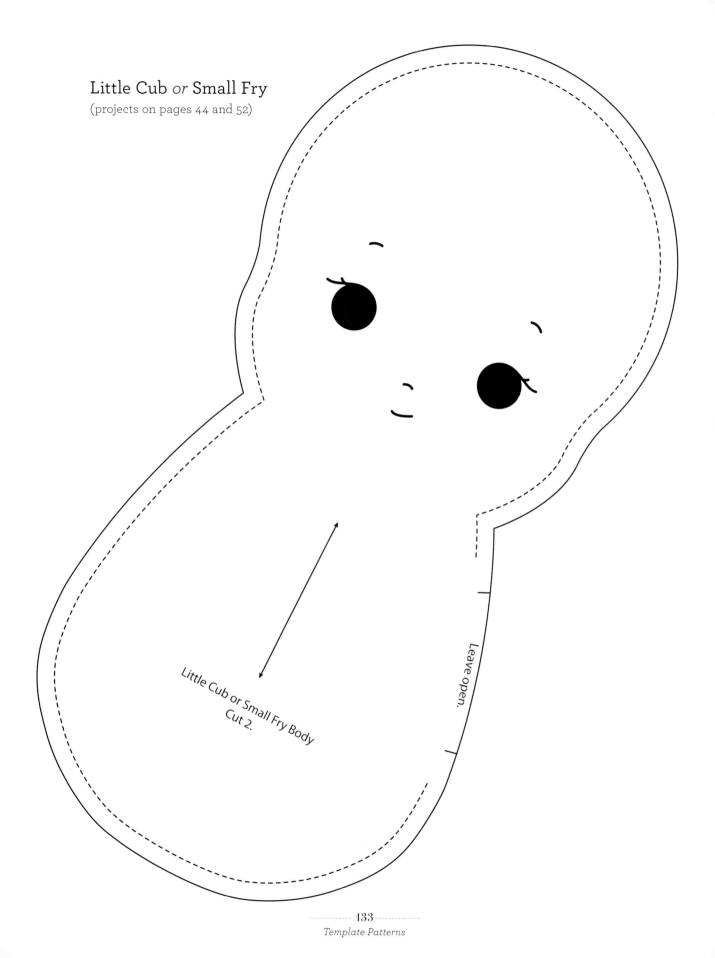

Little Cub *or* Small Fry

(projects on pages 44 and 52)

Little Cub or Small Fry Body
Cut 2.

Leave open.

Template Patterns

Small Fry

(project on page 52)

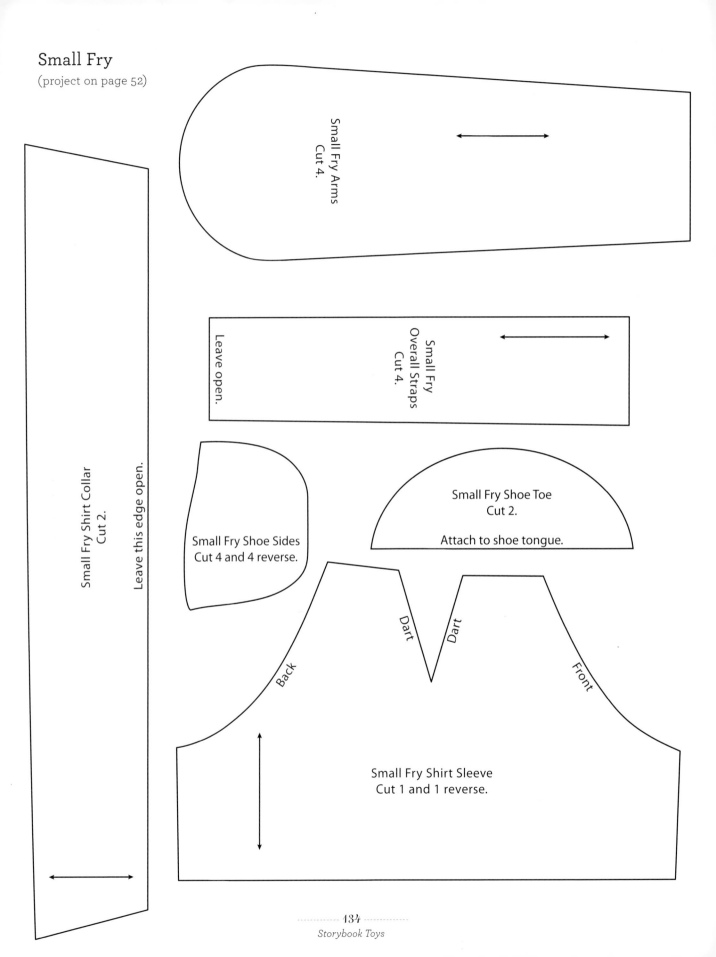

Small Fry Arms
Cut 4.

Small Fry
Overall Straps
Cut 4.

Leave open.

Small Fry Shirt Collar
Cut 2.

Leave this edge open.

Small Fry Shoe Sides
Cut 4 and 4 reverse.

Small Fry Shoe Toe
Cut 2.

Attach to shoe tongue.

Dart

Dart

Back

Front

Small Fry Shirt Sleeve
Cut 1 and 1 reverse.

Small Fry

(project on page 52)

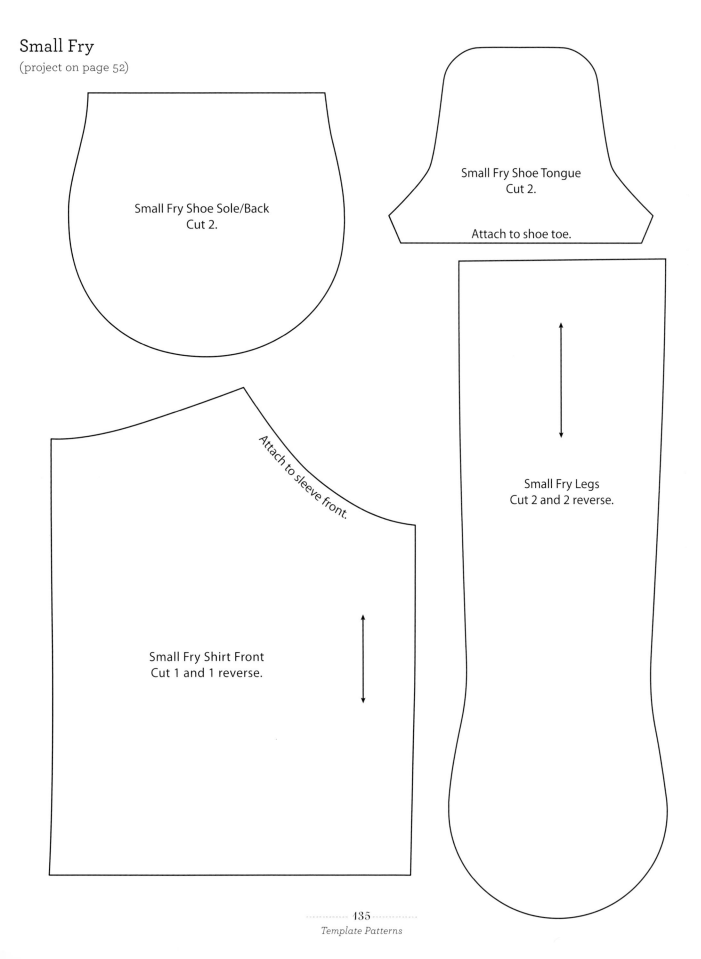

Small Fry Shoe Sole/Back
Cut 2.

Small Fry Shoe Tongue
Cut 2.

Attach to shoe toe.

Attach to sleeve front.

Small Fry Legs
Cut 2 and 2 reverse.

Small Fry Shirt Front
Cut 1 and 1 reverse.

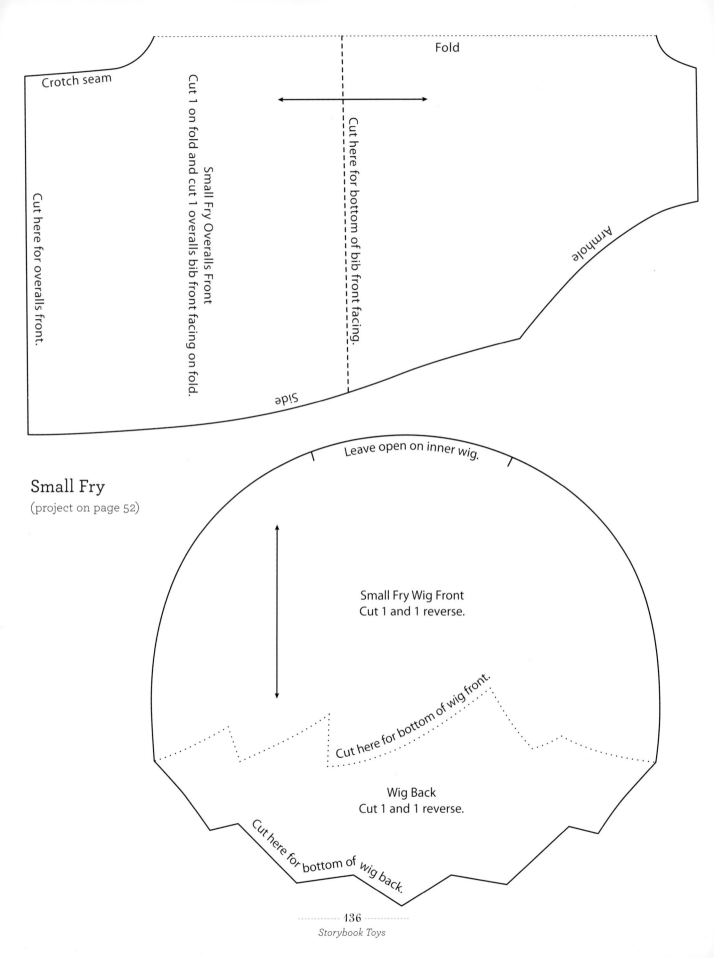

Crotch seam

Fold

Cut here for overalls front.

Small Fry Overalls Front
Cut 1 on fold and cut 1 overalls bib front facing on fold.

Cut here for bottom of bib front facing.

Armhole

Side

Leave open on inner wig.

Small Fry

(project on page 52)

Small Fry Wig Front
Cut 1 and 1 reverse.

Cut here for bottom of wig front.

Wig Back
Cut 1 and 1 reverse.

Cut here for bottom of wig back.

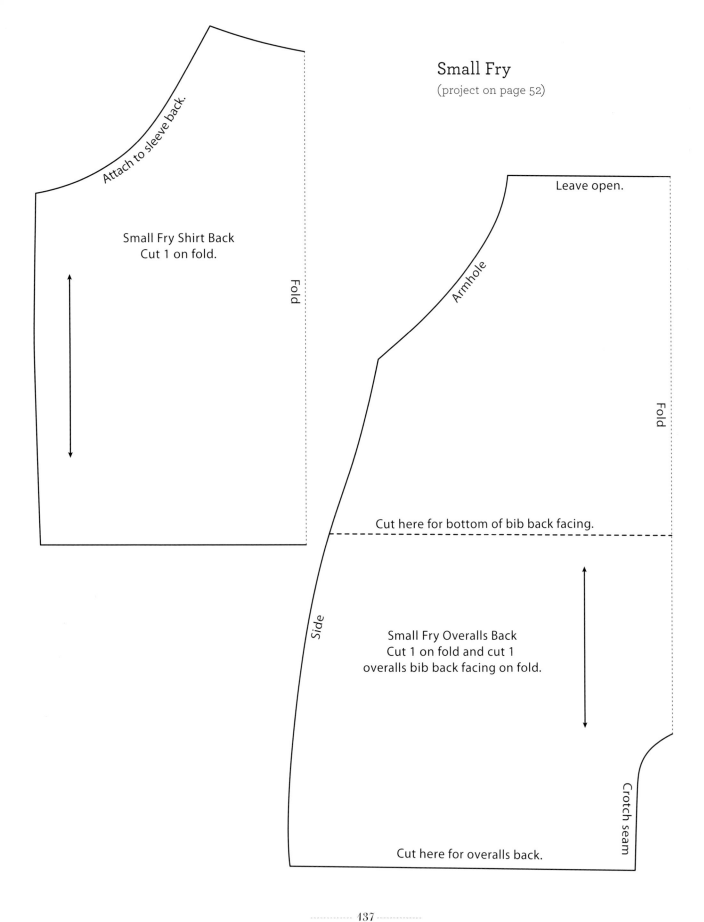

Small Fry
(project on page 52)

Attach to sleeve back.

Small Fry Shirt Back
Cut 1 on fold.

Fold

Leave open.

Armhole

Fold

Cut here for bottom of bib back facing.

Side

Small Fry Overalls Back
Cut 1 on fold and cut 1
overalls bib back facing on fold.

Crotch seam

Cut here for overalls back.

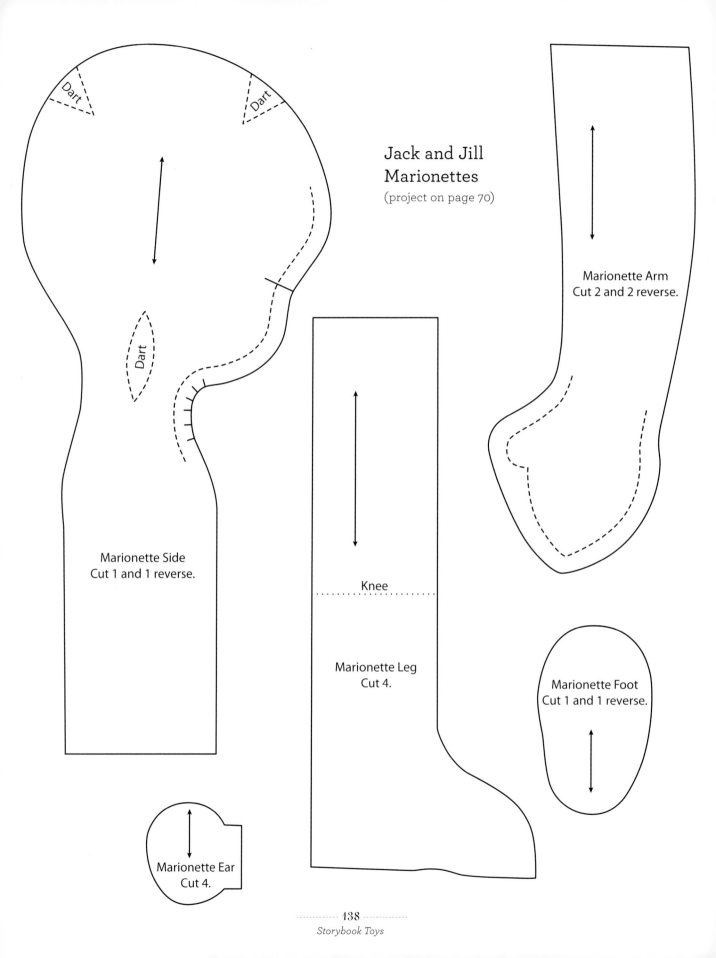

Jack and Jill
Marionettes
(project on page 70)

Marionette Arm
Cut 2 and 2 reverse.

Dart

Dart

Dart

Marionette Side
Cut 1 and 1 reverse.

Knee

Marionette Leg
Cut 4.

Marionette Foot
Cut 1 and 1 reverse.

Marionette Ear
Cut 4.

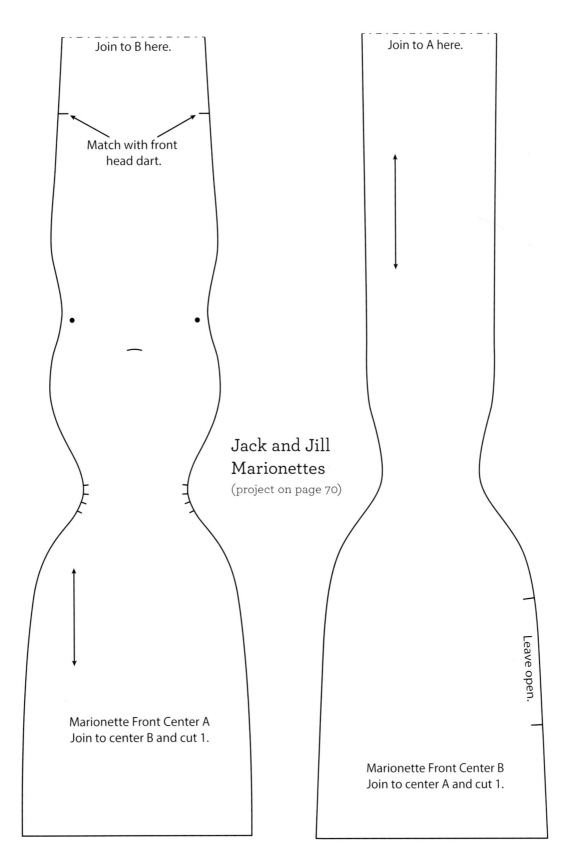

Join to B here.

Join to A here.

Match with front
head dart.

Jack and Jill
Marionettes
(project on page 70)

Leave open.

Marionette Front Center A
Join to center B and cut 1.

Marionette Front Center B
Join to center A and cut 1.

Jack and Jill Marionettes

(project on page 70)

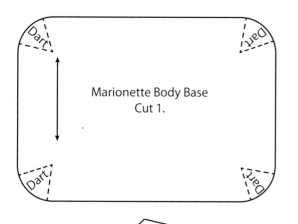

Marionette Body Base
Cut 1.

Marionette Girl Dress Bodice Back
Cut 1 and 1 reverse.

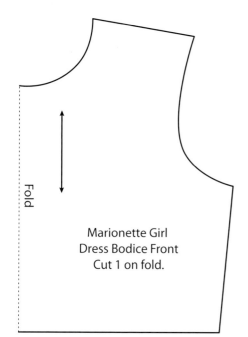

Marionette Girl
Dress Bodice Front
Cut 1 on fold.

Fold

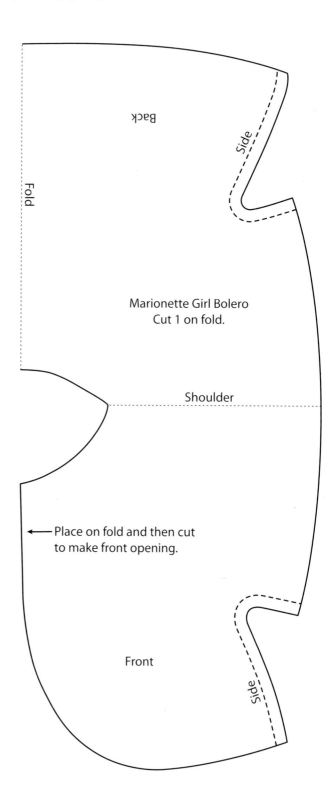

Back

Side

Marionette Girl Bolero
Cut 1 on fold.

Shoulder

← Place on fold and then cut
to make front opening.

Front

Side

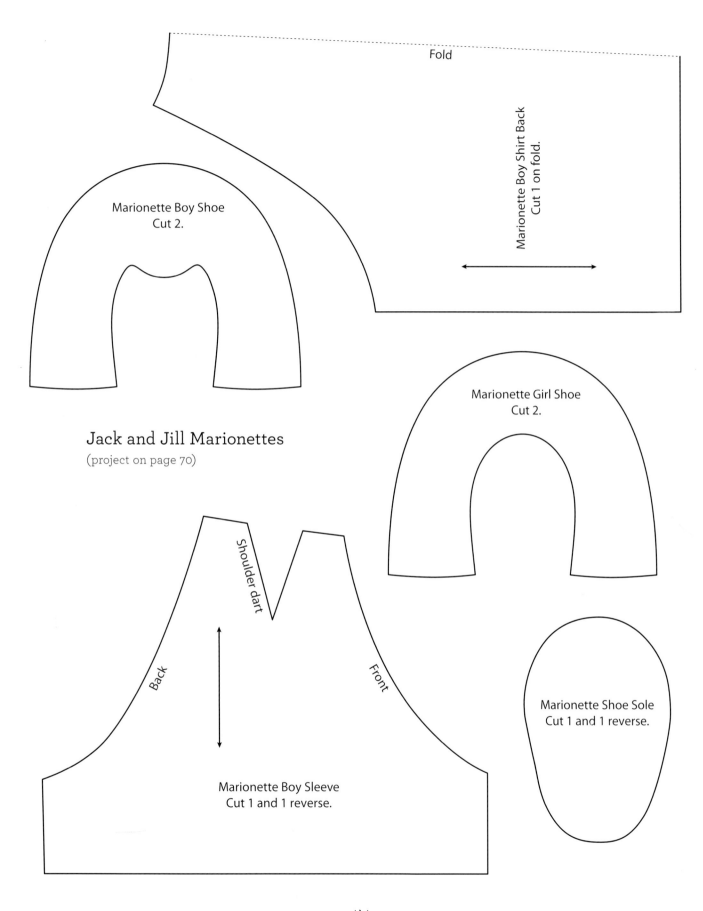

Fold

Marionette Boy Shirt Back
Cut 1 on fold.

Marionette Boy Shoe
Cut 2.

Marionette Girl Shoe
Cut 2.

Jack and Jill Marionettes

(project on page 70)

Shoulder dart

Back

Front

Marionette Boy Sleeve
Cut 1 and 1 reverse.

Marionette Shoe Sole
Cut 1 and 1 reverse.

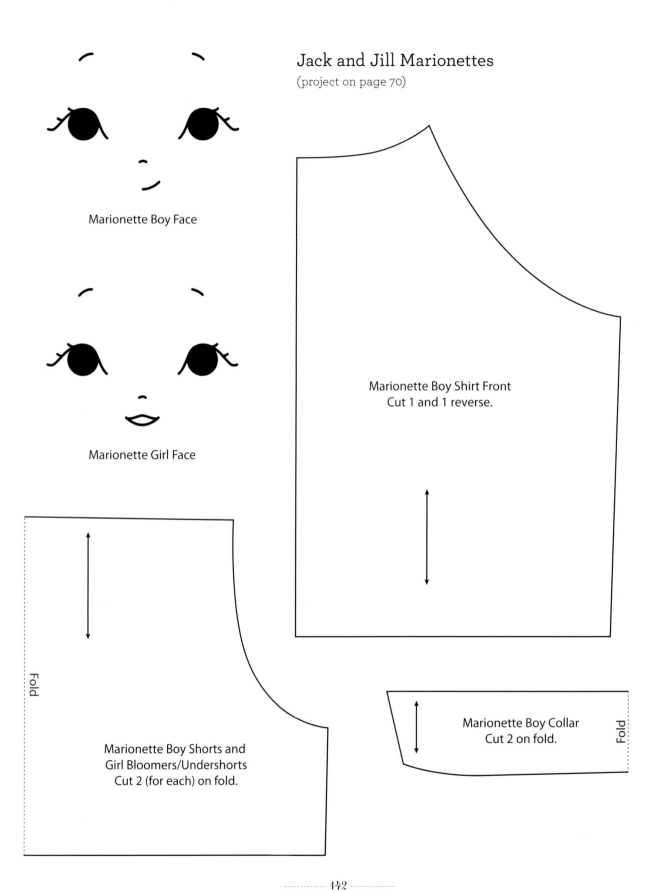

Jack and Jill Marionettes

(project on page 70)

Marionette Boy Face

Marionette Girl Face

Marionette Boy Shirt Front
Cut 1 and 1 reverse.

Marionette Boy Shorts and
Girl Bloomers/Undershorts
Cut 2 (for each) on fold.

Fold

Marionette Boy Collar
Cut 2 on fold.

Fold

Little Red Riding Hood
Puppet Set

(project on page 77)

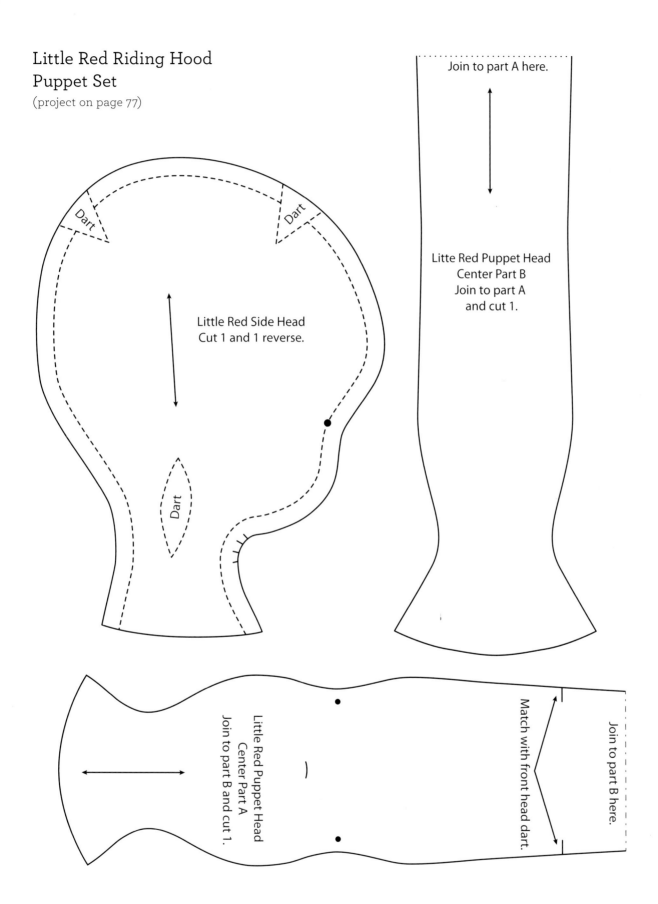

Dart

Dart

Little Red Side Head
Cut 1 and 1 reverse.

Dart

Join to part A here.

Litte Red Puppet Head
Center Part B
Join to part A
and cut 1.

Little Red Puppet Head
Center Part A
Join to part B and cut 1.

Match with front head dart.

Join to part B here.

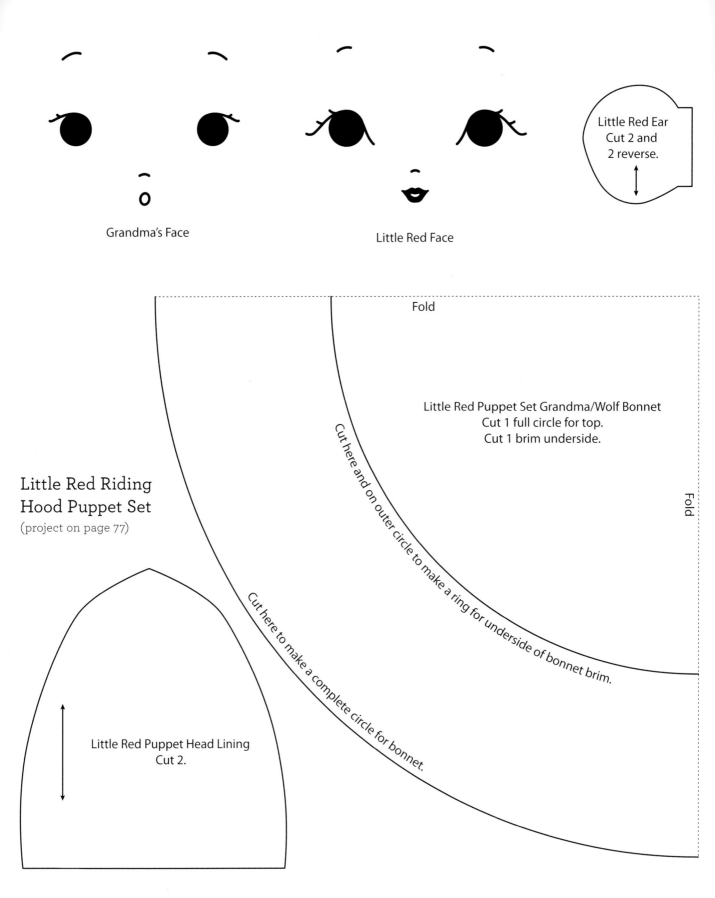

Grandma's Face

Little Red Face

Little Red Ear
Cut 2 and
2 reverse.

Fold

Little Red Puppet Set Grandma/Wolf Bonnet
Cut 1 full circle for top.
Cut 1 brim underside.

Fold

Little Red Riding Hood Puppet Set

(project on page 77)

Cut here and on outer circle to make a ring for underside of bonnet brim.

Cut here to make a complete circle for bonnet.

Little Red Puppet Head Lining
Cut 2.

Little Red Riding Hood Puppet Set

(project on page 77)

Note: *Puppet body pattern located on pullout page P4.*

Little Red Puppet Hands
Cut 2 and 2 reverse for Little Red.
Cut 1 and 1 reverse each
for Grandma and wolf.

Top

Little Red Mushroom Appliqué

Top

Back

Little Red Hood
Cut 1 and 1 outer.
Cut 1 and 1 lining.

Stem

Shoulder dart

Template Patterns

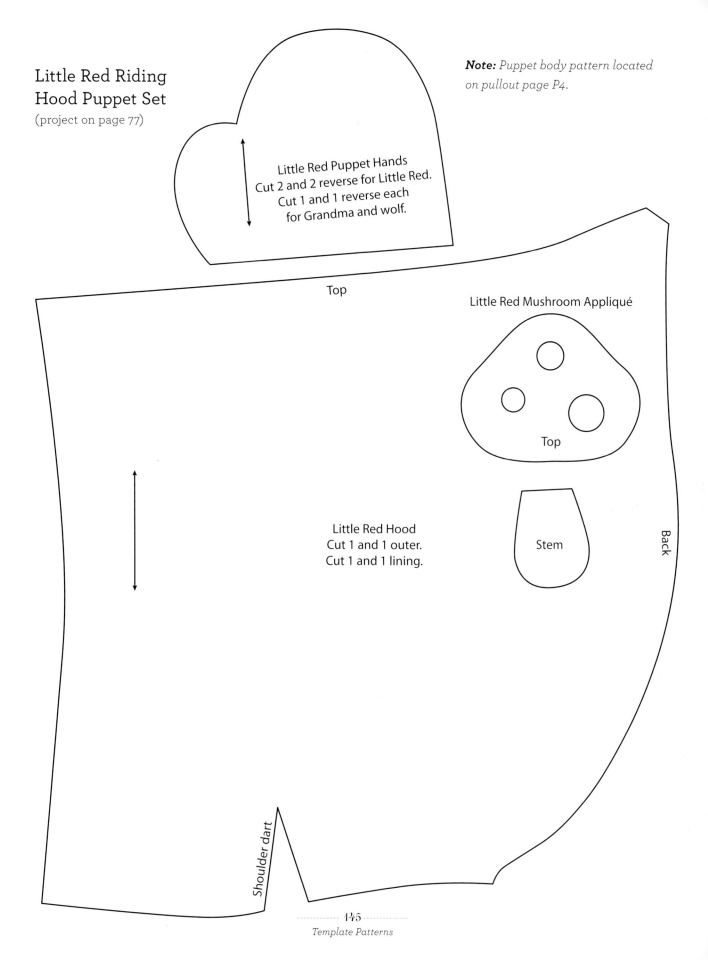

Little Red Riding Hood Puppet Set

(project on page 77)

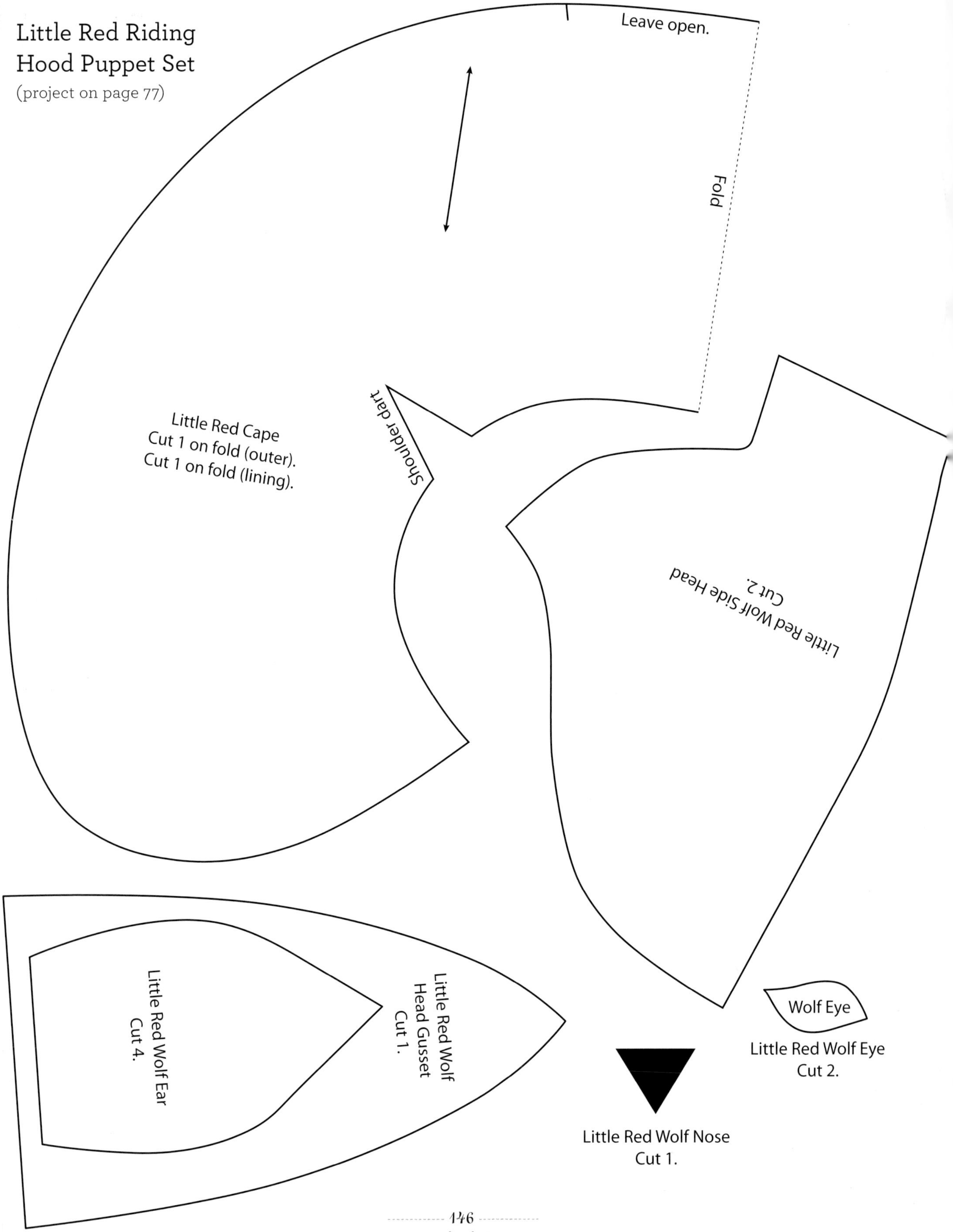

Leave open.

Fold

Little Red Cape
Cut 1 on fold (outer).
Cut 1 on fold (lining).

Shoulder dart

Little Red Wolf Side Head
Cut 2.

Little Red Wolf Ear
Cut 4.

Little Red Wolf Head Gusset
Cut 1.

Wolf Eye

Little Red Wolf Eye
Cut 2.

Little Red Wolf Nose
Cut 1.

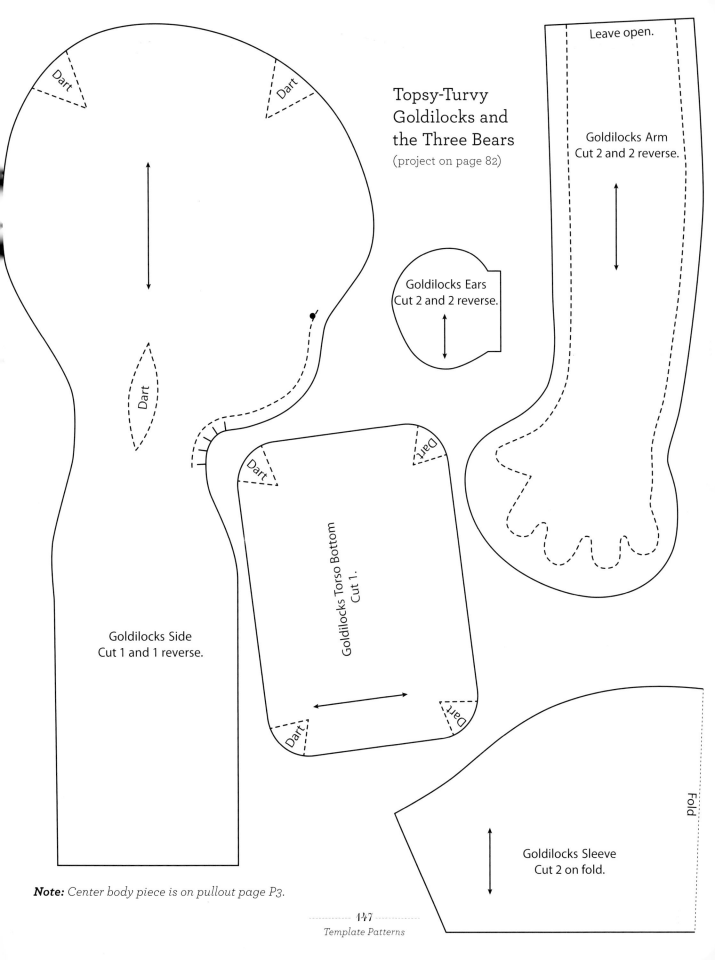

Dart

Dart

Dart

**Topsy-Turvy
Goldilocks and
the Three Bears**

(project on page 82)

Leave open.

Goldilocks Arm
Cut 2 and 2 reverse.

Goldilocks Ears
Cut 2 and 2 reverse.

Dart

Dart

Goldilocks Torso Bottom
Cut 1.

Dart

Dart

Goldilocks Side
Cut 1 and 1 reverse.

Fold

Goldilocks Sleeve
Cut 2 on fold.

Note: *Center body piece is on pullout page P3.*

Template Patterns

Topsy-Turvy Goldilocks and the Three Bears

(project on page 82)

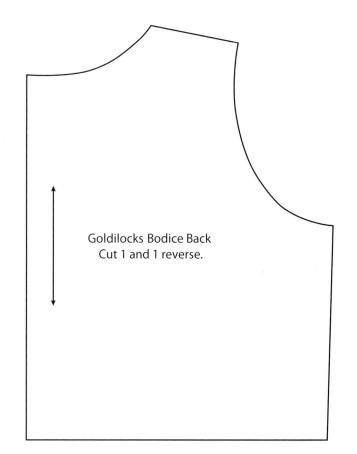

Goldilocks Face

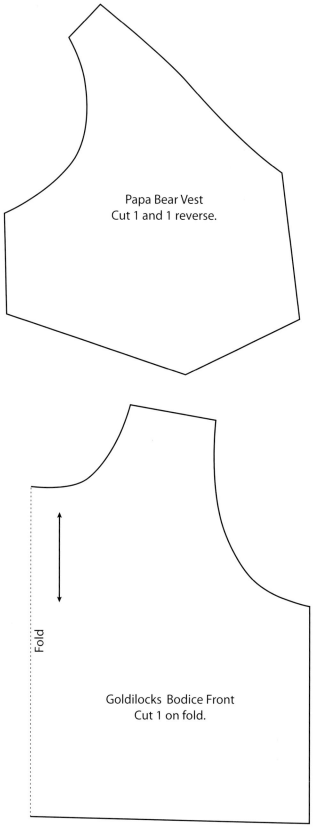

Papa Bear Vest
Cut 1 and 1 reverse.

Goldilocks Bodice Back
Cut 1 and 1 reverse.

Fold

Goldilocks Bodice Front
Cut 1 on fold.

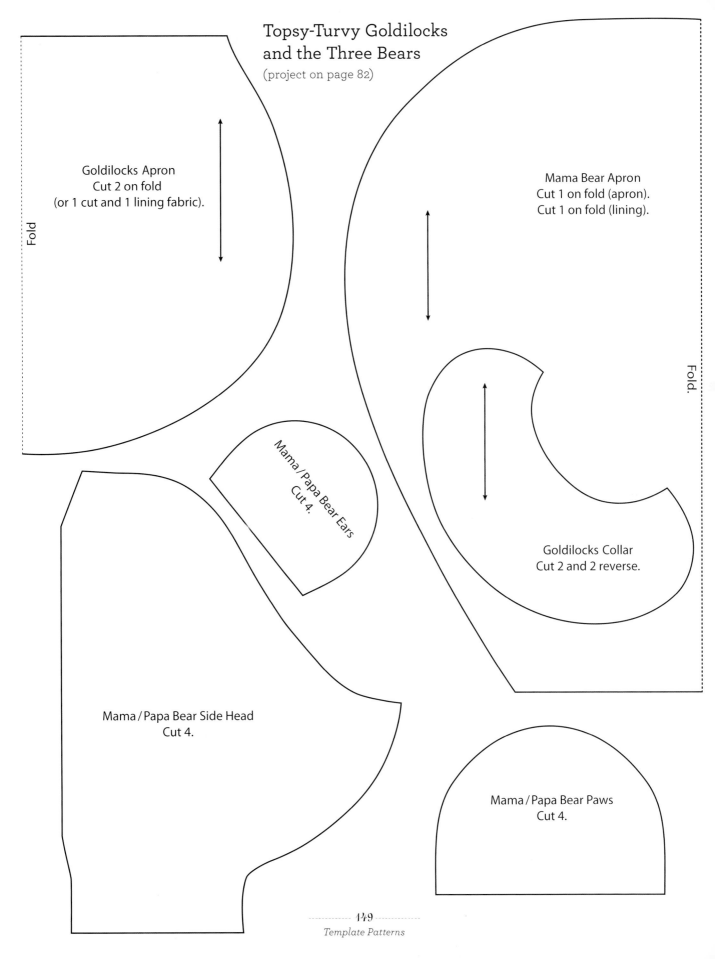

Topsy-Turvy Goldilocks and the Three Bears

(project on page 82)

Goldilocks Apron
Cut 2 on fold
(or 1 cut and 1 lining fabric).

Fold

Mama Bear Apron
Cut 1 on fold (apron).
Cut 1 on fold (lining).

Fold.

Mama / Papa Bear Ears
Cut 4.

Goldilocks Collar
Cut 2 and 2 reverse.

Mama / Papa Bear Side Head
Cut 4.

Mama / Papa Bear Paws
Cut 4.

Template Patterns

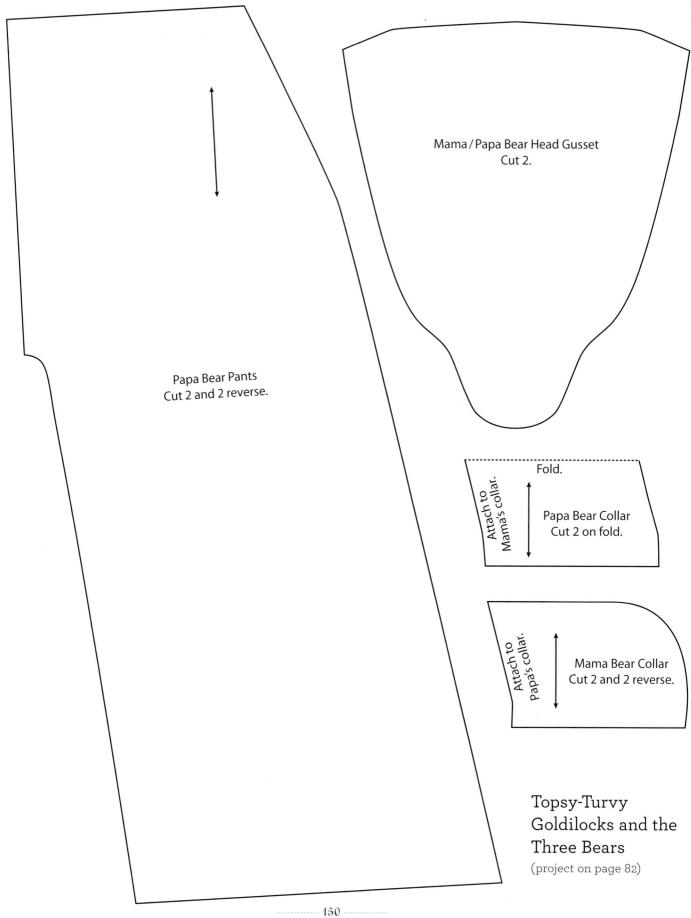

Mama / Papa Bear Head Gusset
Cut 2.

Papa Bear Pants
Cut 2 and 2 reverse.

Fold.

Attach to Mama's collar.

Papa Bear Collar
Cut 2 on fold.

Attach to Papa's collar.

Mama Bear Collar
Cut 2 and 2 reverse.

Topsy-Turvy
Goldilocks and the
Three Bears
(project on page 82)

Topsy-Turvy Goldilocks and the Three Bears

(project on page 82)

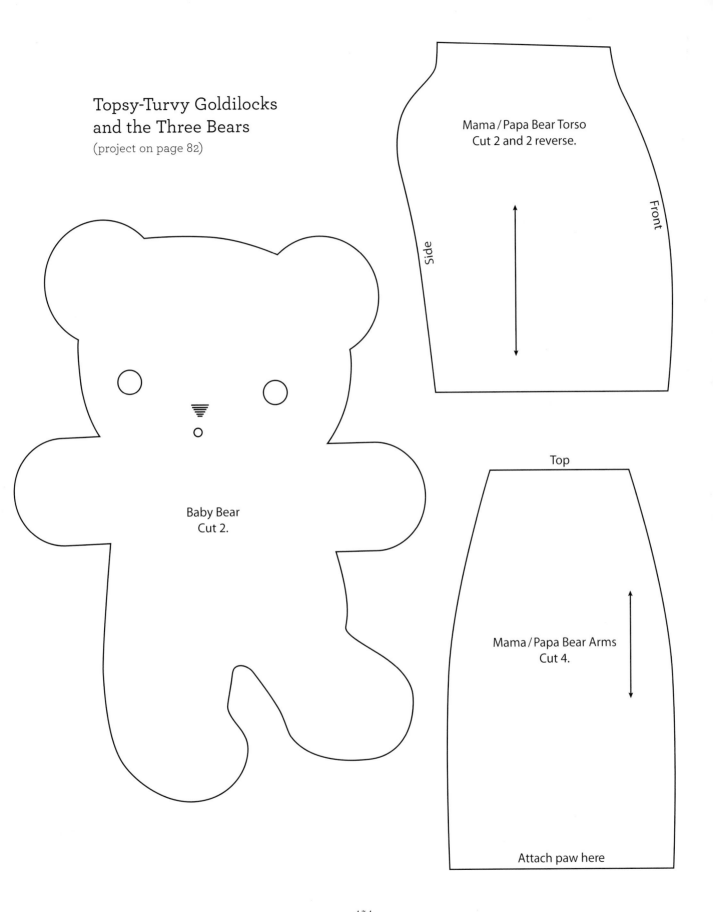

Mama / Papa Bear Torso
Cut 2 and 2 reverse.

Side

Front

Baby Bear
Cut 2.

Top

Mama / Papa Bear Arms
Cut 4.

Attach paw here

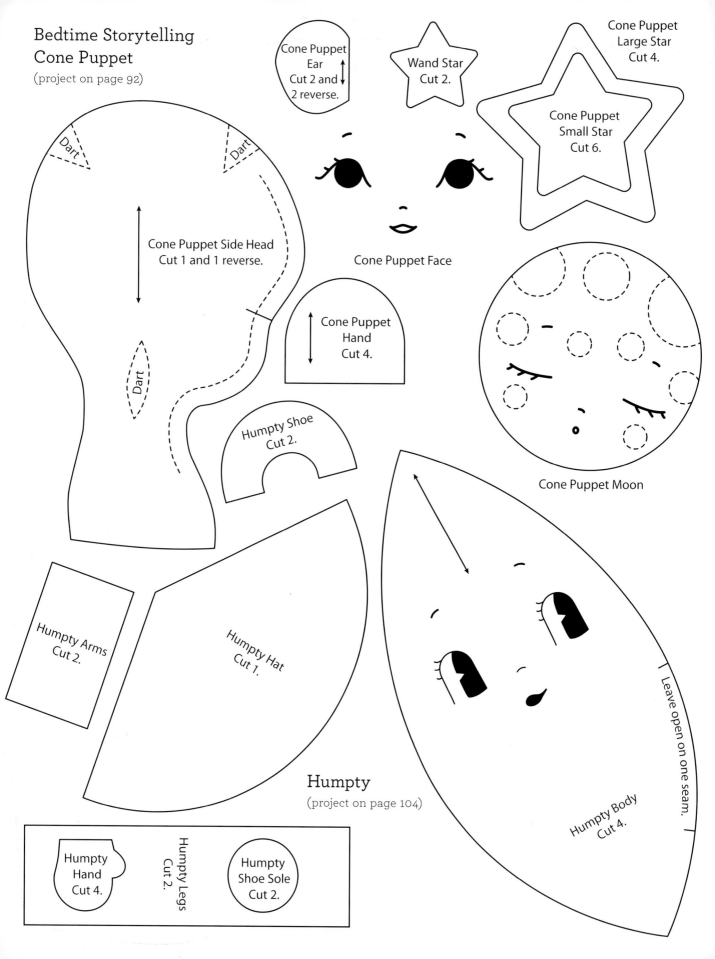

Bedtime Storytelling
Cone Puppet

(project on page 92)

Cone Puppet Ear
Cut 2 and
2 reverse.

Wand Star
Cut 2.

Cone Puppet
Large Star
Cut 4.

Cone Puppet
Small Star
Cut 6.

Dart

Dart

Dart

Cone Puppet Side Head
Cut 1 and 1 reverse.

Cone Puppet Face

Cone Puppet
Hand
Cut 4.

Humpty Shoe
Cut 2.

Cone Puppet Moon

Humpty Arms
Cut 2.

Humpty Hat
Cut 1.

Humpty

(project on page 104)

Leave open on one seam.

Humpty Body
Cut 4.

Humpty
Hand
Cut 4.

Humpty Legs
Cut 2.

Humpty
Shoe Sole
Cut 2.

Little Girl Purse

(project on page 101)

Place purse handles.

Leave open for turning.

Little Girl Purse Outer Lining and Hair and Face Pattern
Cut 1 Face/Front (Wait to cut until after embroidering face.)
Cut 1 back of hair and 1 front of hair (wool felt).
Cut 2 lining (woven cotton).
Cut 2 batting.

Front hair cut and placement line

Place ponytail here.

Place ponytail here.

Leave open on lining only.

Humpty Trousers
Cut 4.

Little Girl Purse Ponytail
Cut 4.

Template Patterns

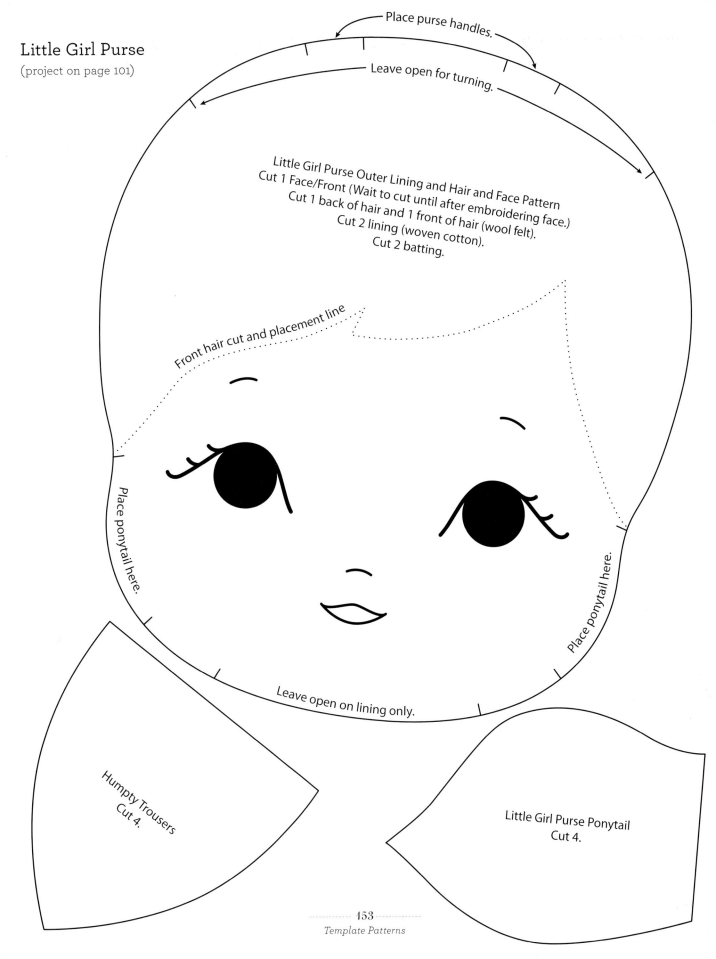

Roly-Poly Duck

(project on page 108)

Back bottom of head

Leave open.

Duck Collar
Cut 2.

Duck Bill
Inside Upper
Cut 1.

Duck Bill Outer

Cut 1.

Duck Center Head Gusset
Cut 1.

Front bottom of head

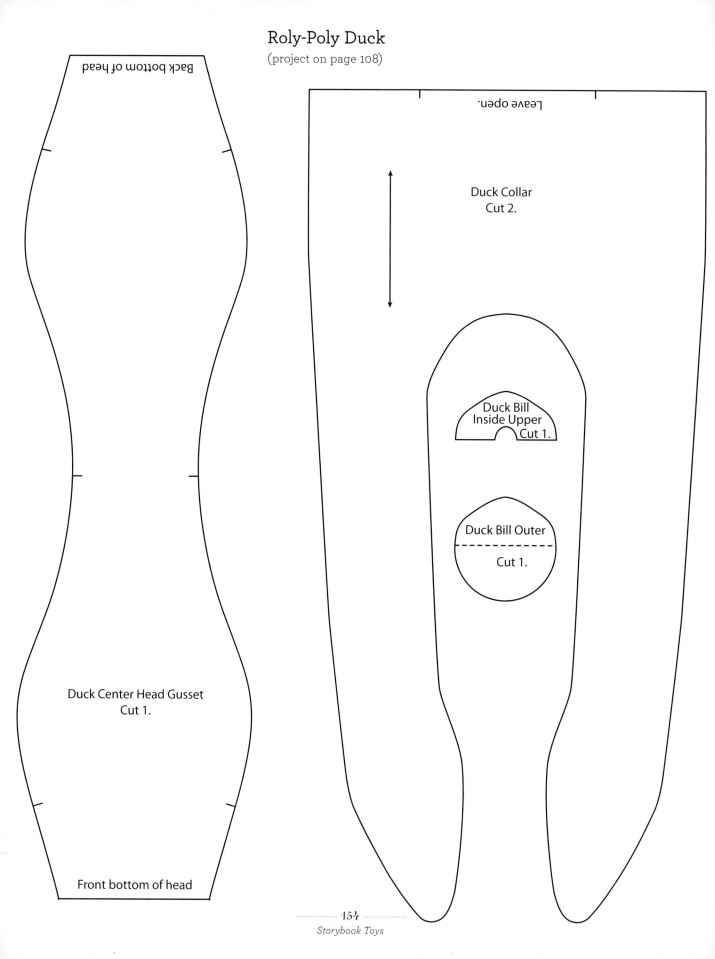

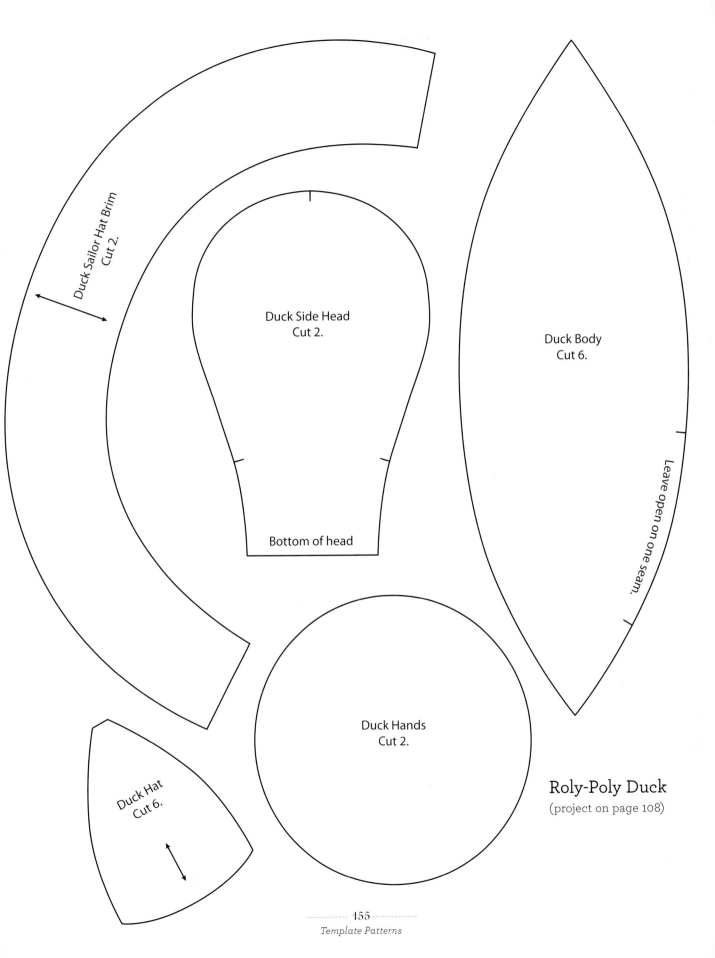

Duck Sailor Hat Brim
Cut 2.

Duck Side Head
Cut 2.

Bottom of head

Duck Body
Cut 6.

Leave open on one seam.

Duck Hands
Cut 2.

Duck Hat
Cut 6.

Roly-Poly Duck

(project on page 108)

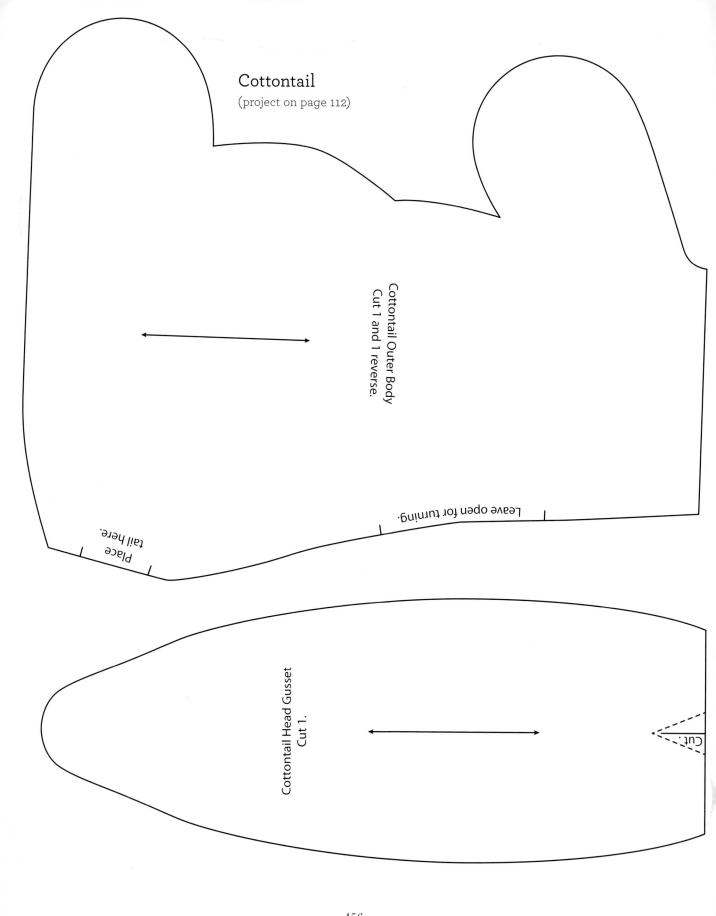

Cottontail

(project on page 112)

Cottontail Outer Body
Cut 1 and 1 reverse.

Leave open for turning.

Place tail here.

Cottontail Head Gusset
Cut 1.

Cut

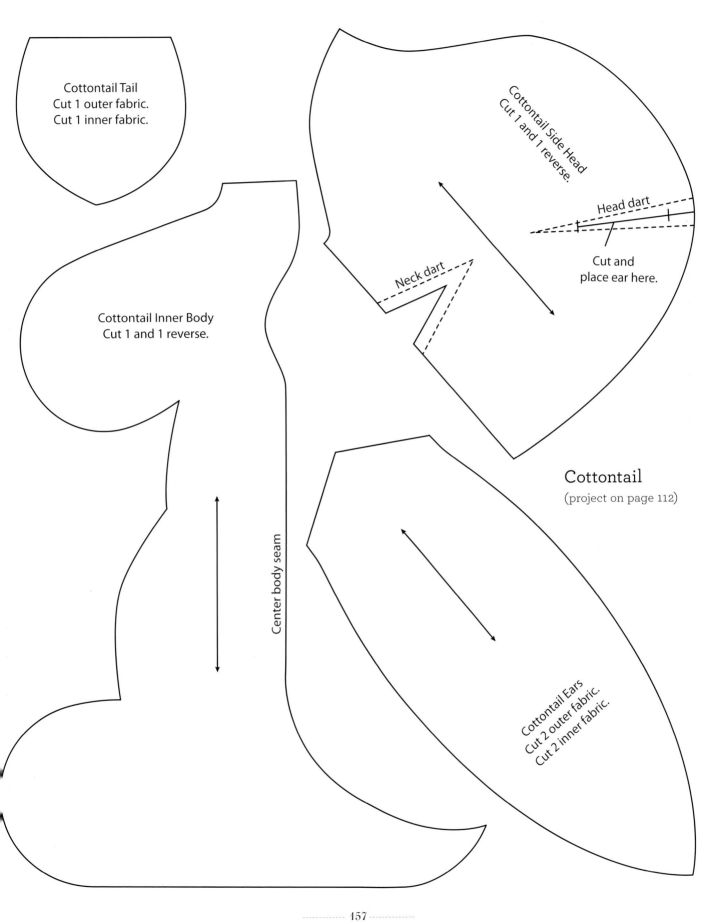

Cottontail Tail
Cut 1 outer fabric.
Cut 1 inner fabric.

Cottontail Side Head
Cut 1 and 1 reverse.

Head dart

Neck dart

Cut and
place ear here.

Cottontail Inner Body
Cut 1 and 1 reverse.

Cottontail
(project on page 112)

Center body seam

Cottontail Ears
Cut 2 outer fabric.
Cut 2 inner fabric.

Elephant Sewing Caddy

(project on page 125)

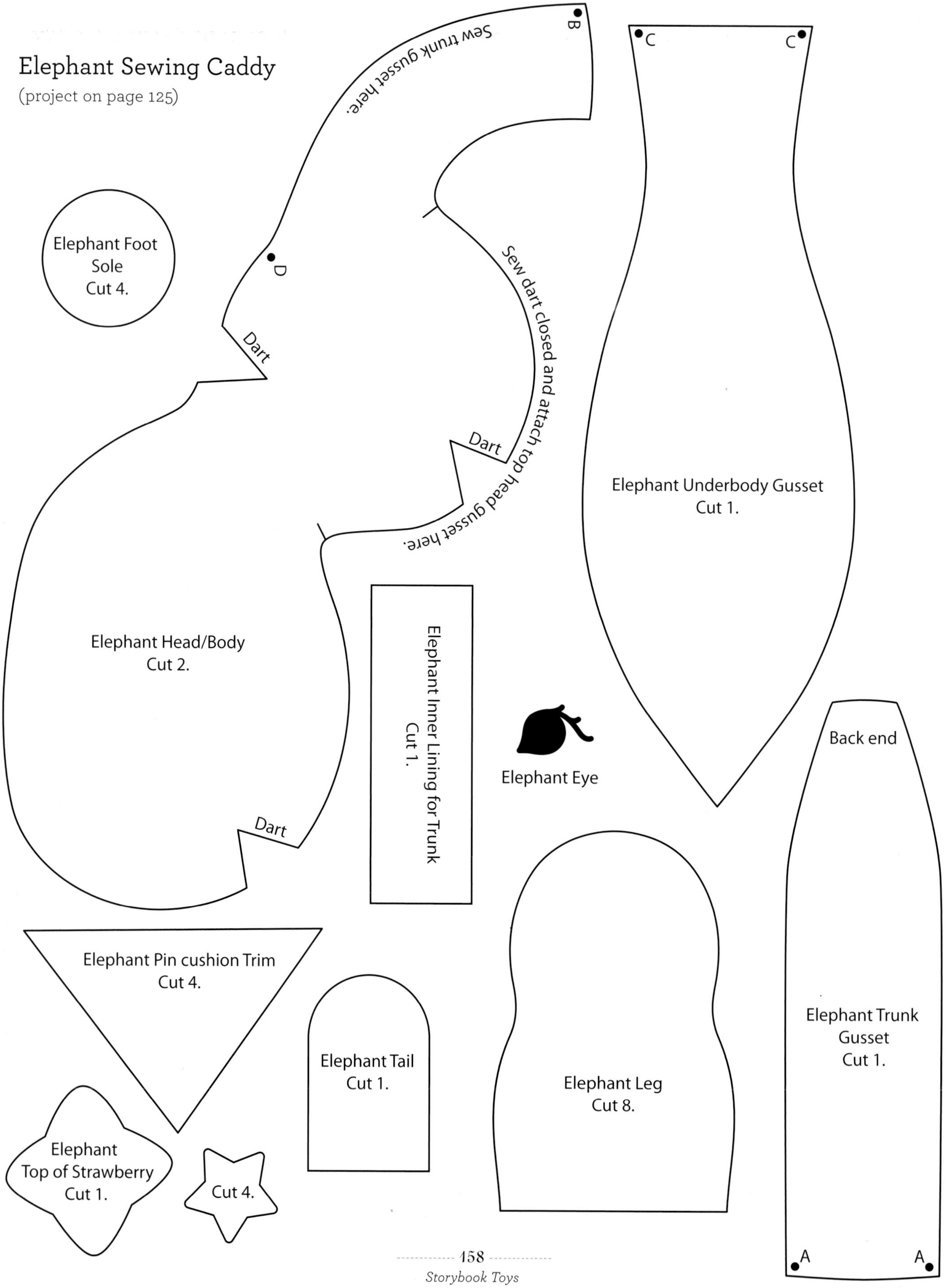

Elephant Foot
Sole
Cut 4.

Sew trunk gusset here.

B

C   C

D

Dart

Sew dart closed and attach top head gusset here.

Dart

Elephant Underbody Gusset
Cut 1.

Elephant Head/Body
Cut 2.

Elephant Inner Lining for Trunk
Cut 1.

Elephant Eye

Back end

Dart

Elephant Pin cushion Trim
Cut 4.

Elephant Tail
Cut 1.

Elephant Leg
Cut 8.

Elephant Trunk
Gusset
Cut 1.

Elephant
Top of Strawberry
Cut 1.

Cut 4.

A   A

Elephant Sewing Caddy

(project on page 125)

Elephant Pin cushion Strip
Cut 1.
Elephant Ear
Cut 4.
Elephant Blankets
Cut 1 on outer line and
1 on inner line.
Elephant Scissors
Holder
Cut 1.
Elephant Pin Cushion Base and Top
Cut 2.
Trunk
Elephant Top Head Gusset
Cut 1.
Dart
Dart
Back of head
Elephant Hat
Cut 1.

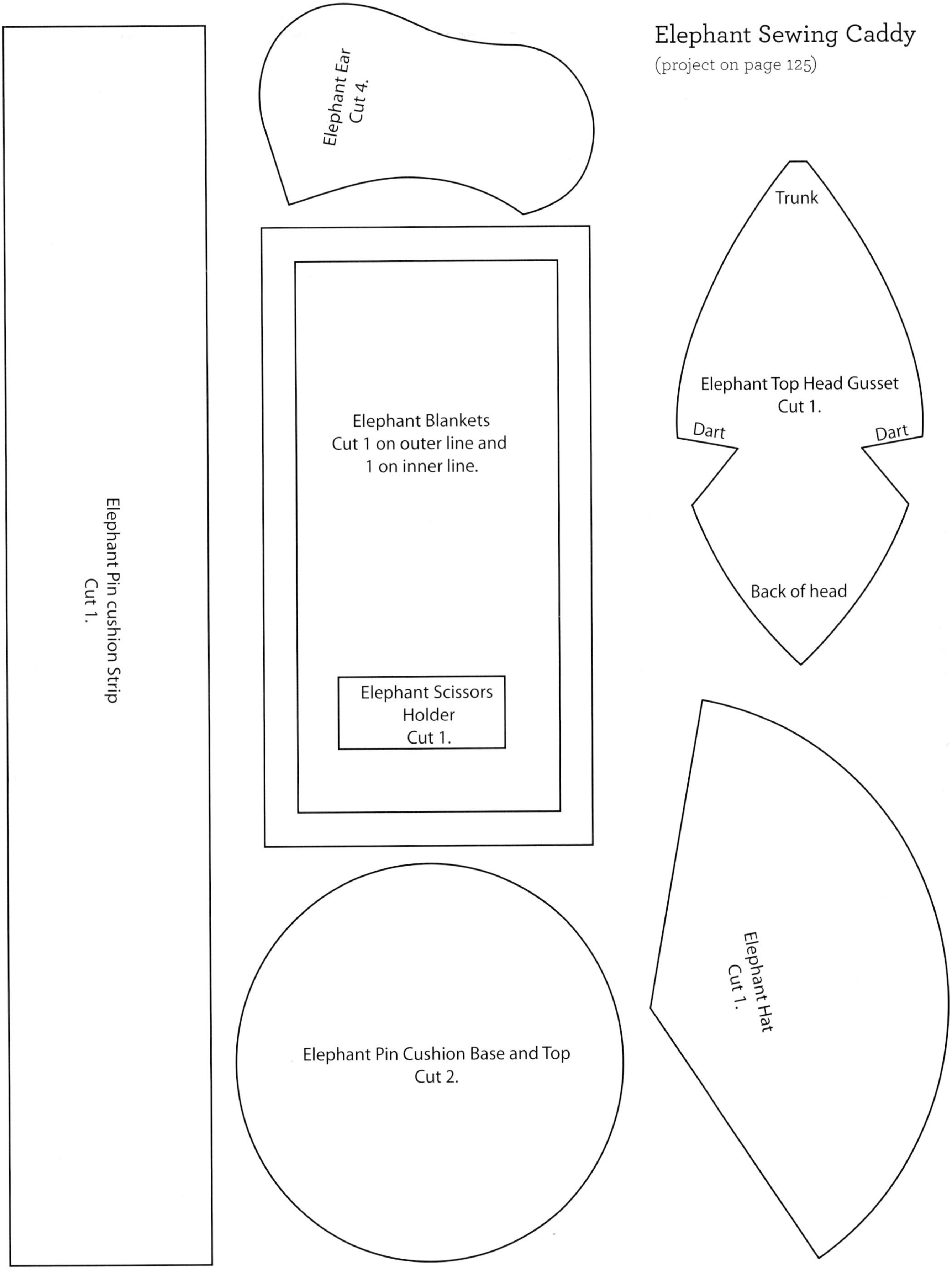

resources

FABRIC AND TRIMS

Etsy
etsy.com

Fabric Worm
fabricworm.com

Fat Quarter Shop
fatquartershop.com

Harts Fabric
hartsfabric.com

Purl Soho
purlsoho.com

Sew, Mama, Sew
sewmamasew.com

Superbuzzy
superbuzzy.com

WOOL FELT AND STUFFING

A Child's Dream Come True
(wool felt and stuffing)
achildsdream.com

Etsy
etsy.com

Magic Cabin
(wool felt and stuffing)
magiccabin.com

Near Sea Naturals
(wool, cotton, and hemp stuffing)
nearseanaturals.com

Weir Dolls and Crafts
(wool felt and stuffing)
weirdollsandcrafts.com

NOTIONS

C&T Publishing
(Timtex)
ctpub.com

YARN AND NEEDLEWORK SUPPLIES

Brown Sheep Company
brownsheep.com

Jimmy Beans Wool
jimmybeanswool.com

Old World Designs
oldworlddesigns.com

DOLL AND MARIONETTE STANDS

Fish River Crafts
(marionette stands and kits)
fishriver.com

Magic Cabin
(saddle-style doll stands)
magiccabin.com

about the author

Jill Hamor grew up in Southern California loving animals, drawing prolifically, and playing soccer with her sisters and brother. She completed her undergraduate degree at UCLA and received an MPH in health policy from UC Berkeley, after which she worked to promote access to quality health care in California.

Jill is a newcomer to handcrafting, inspired to design, sew, and knit over the past eight years for her three daughters and her nieces and nephews. She now resides in the San Francisco Bay Area with her family and their newest addition, Lily the black lab mix. You can find more of Jill's work at her blog, bybido.blogspot.com.